"A thorough and sensitive look at expat life that provides caring and practical advice, allowing expat spouses and families to thrive. Hats off to the authors for sharing their vast experience and valuable lessons learned."

Lisa Kessler, PhD, RD,
Interim Dean, Huntley College of Agriculture

"An absolute primer to easily reference along your sometimes bumpy road to expat living. While no one will ever be an expert at transitions, this book is a valuable tool to help gauge your expectations and emotions as you transition through your cycle of mobility in your expat lifestyle."

Becky Henderson,
CLO Coordinator, US Embassy Oman

"Exhale expats, you have the experts on your side! This wonderfully organized gem of a book is full of practical ideas, encouragement, wisdom, and humor to help you proceed with confidence through an international move and beyond."

Kate Casey, LPC, JD.
Autumn Ridge Counseling and Wellness

"This book and pragmatic guide for the whole relocation process hits the nail on the head. Most importantly it sheds much-needed light on one of the crucial factors of global mobility and relocation – the spousal situation."

Håkan Rantakeisu,
Founder of Grow Internationals, growinternationals.com

"Fantastic book I wish I had read before starting my life as an expat more than 20 years ago. Written in an easy-to-read style with tales contributed by expats living around the world, sharing their experiences of growth and discovery. A must-read and a crucial tool to ensure present survival, adaptation and future fulfillment in your decision to become a global citizen. Great job, ladies!"

"What a fantastic guide through the complexities of setting up a life in a new country. A must-read for every spouse embarking on a phenomenally rewarding but complex expat journey. Whether a newbie or a seasoned expat, you will feel the authors' experience, warmth and wisdom emanating from these pages."

"Having assisted thousands of expat families relocating to Sweden, we generally know who will have a smooth expatriation and who will not. The companies should make this easy-to-read guidebook mandatory reading for the families they send abroad. Straightforward tips from experienced expats."

"*Best friend and travel expert in one – this sage advice helps anyone navigate major change with awareness, creativity and humor. Use these insights to lighten what can be a heavy experience by finding the freeing and positive opportunities that come with life as an expat!*"

Jennifer Quarrie,
International creativity, wellness and innovation strategist

"*As a Foreign Service Officer and former military officer, I thoroughly enjoyed this book and found it applicable for both working and non-working expats. The optimistic outlook and ideas for handling the challenges and difficulties of living abroad were refreshing. I strongly recommend this book for anyone about to take the exciting step of living in a foreign country. Enjoy the adventures!*"

Sara Mann,
US Foreign Service Officer, former US military officer

Unpack
A Guide to Life as an Expat Spouse

by Lana Wimmer and Tanya Arler

Unpack: A Guide to Life as an Expat Spouse

Co-Authored by Lana Wimmer and Tanya Arler

First published in Great Britain 2017
by Springtime Books

© Lana Wimmer and Tanya Arler

Cover and interior pages designed by:
Owen Jones Design   owenjonesdesign.com

ISBN: 978-0-9932377-8-2

Dedicated to the countless expat
spouses who have gone before us
to pave the way, and to the countless
who will follow.

Acknowledgements

If not for our expat journey – and one another – this book never would have been written. *Unpack: A Guide to Life as an Expat Spouse* represents a true amalgamation of our hearts and minds. Expat friends rock!

We also couldn't have done it without the support of the most important people in our lives: our husbands and children. They inspired us throughout our expat journey and were our biggest supporters, cheering us on and celebrating our smallest of "wins" when we overcame obstacles. Without them, let's be honest, we wouldn't even be here. So for that, they get a big thank you and a home cooked dinner.

Okay, drumroll please... for our biggest and loudest shout out, a HUGE big, big, big thank you goes to all the amazing expat women who contributed their very own real life stories to this book. You are brave and courageous and illuminate this work in a way nothing else could. Thank you Kayla Carter, Sarah Davies, Clare Doyle, Simone Esman, Nancy Johnson, Martha Klinger, Kathleen L'Esperance, Elizabeth Linder, Hallie Marcellus, Soledad Matteozzi, Pyper McIntosh, Linda

Mueller, Sandy Nylund, Frederica Rossi, Alexa Servante, Yael Shoham and Misty Wright.

We also want to thank Clare Doyle, Elayne Wells Harmer, Keri-Lynn Kendall and Heleen Kist from the top to the very bottom of our hearts for reading early versions of our manuscript and giving us feedback. You not only made this work better, you bolstered our spirits and for that we will never forget you.

When it was all said, and mostly done, we looked for just the right publisher. Thank you to the entire Springtime Books team for believing in our project and being just as certain, if not more, that it could all come together inside one great cover.

Table of Contents

Part II On the Move

Part III Daily Life

Part IV Family Dynamics

Part V Expat Friendships

Part VI The Next Move

Continuing the Conversation

About the Authors

Preface

So here you are. Your husband's work is moving the whole family to a new country and the thought of packing up your home and transporting you and your kids into a whole new world is exciting and anxiety-provoking at the same time.

You're worried about the kids and the logistics of it all, not to mention wondering what life will be like once you get there. If you've never done anything like this before it can feel daunting.

Wouldn't it be great if you could wave a magic wand and someone would appear who could tell you what to expect and how to handle the inevitable twists and turns that lie on the road ahead?

Well, ta-da, this is your magic wand. *Sort of.* Only we won't appear in person while you sit there in your jammies reading. (That might be scary for all of us.) But you'll feel like we're right there with you, as you read the dilemmas and advice we'll be sharing in *Unpack: A Guide to Life as an Expat Spouse* to help you navigate your expat journey.

We wrote this book because we know what you need most is something you can read on the go or when the going gets tough – a book with straightforward answers. Expat life is busy and overwhelming in the beginning, so we've designed *Unpack: A Guide to Life as an Expat Spouse* to be read cover to cover or to pick up any time for some quick inspiration.

How do we know? Because between the two of us we've made fifteen international moves spanning three continents. That's a lot of schlepping around! And through it all we've learned invaluable universal lessons and will share advice that will help you, regardless of where your new home is in the world.

With this simple, practical advice you can avoid common expat mishaps and get right into enjoying the adventure. We'll help you with things such as... how to build a support system, find the best place to live, choose the right schools and activities for your kids, support your spouse, and do everything it takes to settle your family into a new country and create a life for yourself.

Whether you're starting your first move overseas or have been in town a while – but still can't get the hang of it – pick up this book, flip to any page and find thought-provoking ideas and encouragement for your journey.

Moving to a new country requires a lot of unpacking, not only your boxes, but your life too. With this guide (aka magic wand) in hand, *Unpack: A Guide to Life as an Expat Spouse* will help you with the heavy lifting.

Part I
Starting Out

1. What the heck is an expat?

My husband just told me the company might move us to Timbuktu and offered us an "expat" package. What the heck is an expat and is that something I even want to be?

———

Hold on, help is on the way.

"Expat" is short for "expatriate." It means, "a person who lives outside their native country." And you're reading a book written by two of them. But if you ask us what it is... well it's much, *much* more!

Becoming an expat means you take on a whole new lifestyle.

When you start out you might be anxious, excited, nervous or shy, but we've found that once you get into the groove, being an expat means you become universally more adventurous and curious about cultures and places. You'll open yourself up to the world and learn to be comfortable exploring it.

Expats discover stepping out of their comfort zone doesn't have to be terrifying. They seize opportunities and are continually expanding their horizons.

As co-authors of this book we've each had very different expat experiences, but we both love the choices we've made. That doesn't mean it hasn't been a roller coaster, we've had our ups and downs. But along the way we've learned to make the most of our expat journeys. We'll be sharing our real-life advice and hands-on solutions here, to help you make the most of your life as an expat.

Regardless of your posting or situation, there are universal truths to help ease your entry into this great adventure, so keep reading. You're going to figure this out.

OUR ADVICE
Becoming an expat means you embark on an adventure of a lifetime!

___

WORDS TO REMEMBER

'To live will be an awfully big adventure.'

Peter Pan in *Peter Pan*, J.M. Barrie

___

2. Do we turn our world upside down?

I've researched websites and browsed travel blogs, but I still don't know if I want to live the expat life. Do I want to leave my friends and family behind? Can I handle a move to another country?

We understand that it's one thing to dream about living in a new country, but a whole other kettle of fish to pack up and move everything you own. We won't lie to you, *it's big*. But if you can handle a little bit of adventure, you can manage this and will even grow to love it.

Yes, you could stay in your comfort zone, but if you don't take the chance to step out you'll never expand your worldview, travel to exotic places, or gain new perspectives on... well, everything.

We hear what you might be saying, "Do I really *need* to change my worldview?" Maybe not. But the world is expanding at a phenomenal rate and here's your opportunity to see it differently. Take this as our gentle nudge to say, *don't pass it up*.

It's challenging to adapt to a new lifestyle and culture, but with a little flexibility you'll learn to handle far more than you'd suspect. Saying goodbye to friends and family is difficult, but this is not "goodbye" forever.

You're about to expand your world *and* your friends' and family's world too. This is an opportunity for everyone in your circle of influence to adapt and grow. You'll miss the folks from back home, but given time you'll learn how to be there and support one another in a different way.

If you base your decision solely on what's *easiest* to do in life, you'll miss out on meaningful experiences and what makes the world exciting – the variety. If you have the opportunity to discover new cultures, new friendships, and new ideas with your family, why not do it? Say YES!

OUR ADVICE
Opportunities like this don't come along every day. Your family back home will take this journey with you in their own way, and you'll be expanding their worldview too.

WORDS TO REMEMBER

'It's better to look back on life and say: I can't believe I did that, than to look back and say: I wish I did that.'

Anonymous

---

3. Is it fair to turn our kids' world upside down?

My kids have lots of friends at school and in our neighborhood. We're comfortable here and close to family. Should I make them change everything because I want to move? Is it fair to take them away from what's familiar and plunge them into the unknown?

As a parent it's your job to set boundaries, enforce bedtimes, make curfews, teach manners, and decide what to feed your children for dinner.

This move is just another one of those choices you'll make to shape your child's future. It's not about what's fair or unfair. There are no good or bad choices here, just *different* choices and they're both okay.

Moving abroad will open their world up to new possibilities and turn them into global citizens. Staying home will give them a different childhood experience, one that is constant and filled with its own challenges. Like anything else you decide for your children, this choice has to be based on what's important to you.

Expat children will come to view the world differently. They don't live next door to the same girl or boy their whole childhood, nor do they add a new mark to the kitchen door every time they grow a couple of inches. Your kids will learn to cross cultural barriers and travel the world confidently, knowing that the unknown doesn't need to be scary.

It's a unique way to grow up in the world. If you value that, then don't worry about the "fairness" of the situation. Kids don't think it's fair to have to eat broccoli either, but it's good for them.

OUR ADVICE
It isn't fair or unfair. It's a choice that will shape them, define their perspective on the world, and give them tools that will serve them throughout their lives.

From those who have been there

An expat story

"How could my parents not hear what I had been repeatedly saying for months, I do not want to move!

I could not believe my parents were moving me halfway across the world from the city I grew up in, the place where I built friendships, was surrounded by family, and created all my memories. The fear of the unknown cluttered my brain for months.

My parents tried to explain that as I would be attending an international school, the kids were used to having new kids and would be super outgoing and accepting. I wasn't buying it.

Luckily, my mom found a buddy program at the school I would be attending, which put me in touch with a girl who would be in my grade. I messaged back and forth with her a few times, which seemed to calm my nerves.

Although I cried the whole flight, we finally made the big jump to our new home country. The first week I felt like we were simply on a family vacation but, to my dismay, I had to start school.

On the first day I left my house with my head down, circling with thoughts. However, I returned home that day with my head held high and a smile across my face. Despite the fact other students had their friend groups formed, they were warm and welcoming towards me. They made me feel as if I was already one of them. This was such a relief to both my parents and me.

Because people come and go frequently at international schools, they have activities in place that allow the new students to establish relationships with their new peers. At our school we had grade level trips. Each grade goes somewhere within the country during the second week of school to bond with their classmates and to experience the local culture. Although my mom was a nervous wreck, this was honestly the best thing that happened to me.

The trip not only allowed me to get to know my new classmates, but also gave them a chance to get to know me. With the foundation for the year set, I had my mind on the future of my time here, rather than weeping over my life in the United States.

Three years later I am still living abroad, with a completely different mindset. The opportunities and relationships I have built here are one of a kind and will be something I carry my whole life. I am only sixteen, yet my adventures have already taught me much more than textbooks and teachers. Leaving my hometown was hard, but it opened eyes and made me realize the many opportunities the world has in store."

Hallie Marcellus — 10th grade student
American/Canadian, lives in Sweden

4. Telling the kids

My husband and I are ready to say "yes," but we aren't quite sure when or how to tell the kids. Do we include them in the decision or do we wait to tell them until after the contract is signed?

If you can wait to share information about the move, hold off until after the contract is signed, particularly if your children are younger. It's best not to burden them too soon, and don't mention it *at all* if you're unsure the contract will be final.

Three months before the move is a good time to share *"the news."* This gives ample lead-time for questioning, goodbyes and packing. Any longer and your kids might find reasons to struggle, and shorter can be a bit of a shock.

Keep in mind that the minute you mention moving, it's done and you can't undo it. If you're lucky your kids will react with excitement, but be prepared for emotional responses such as anger or sadness. It doesn't mean they don't want to go, it's just their initial response to change. Your heart might break to see them upset, but their first response is often based on fears and anxieties that don't reflect how happy they'll be when they get there.

If you want to include your children in the decision process, be sure to consider their age, maturity and temperament. Are they able to see the pros and cons and contribute to a discussion? Do you really want them to have a vote? You might be asking for more upheaval than you bargained for.

Either way, whenever you choose to tell the kids, pick a moment when family members are all together – you want them to hear the news from you. Lead with information to spark their particular interests. If they love animals, talk about the local species. If they're into music and art, emphasize the city's culture. Highlight the positives and most likely they'll pick up on your enthusiasm. If they're old enough for social media try lining up connections with kids their age. Positive reviews from peers go a long way toward easing anxieties and getting them on board with the coming move.

OUR ADVICE
Growing up brings enough uncertainty for children to worry about so avoid creating more. Wait until the contract is signed to announce the move.

An expat story

"We were quite worried to tell our boys about the move to Copenhagen. We planned to tell them Saturday morning to have the weekend to pick up the pieces and mop up the sadness and tears that were going to ensue. We psyched ourselves up and gave the boys a great pancake breakfast.

Honestly, I felt sick. How could I break it to them? So we told them.

Noah's response: 'Can I play football?' Yes. 'Can I have another pancake?' Yes. 'Can we go to Legoland again?' Yes. Then Thomas: 'Right, are we going swimming now?' I, on the other hand, was a complete mess.

Their first day in the new school was amazing. Thomas came home with three best friends and Noah cried because he couldn't stay all day. Honestly they were amazing and by the end of the week it was like they'd been there forever.

Children are fantastically resilient, and we see it time and time again. I think they take their cue from their parents and the biggest conclusion we have come to since moving abroad is that it doesn't matter which house or country we live in, it's just that wherever we are together is home. Bit slushy and openly emotional for Brits but it's true."

Sarah Davies – Head of Everything at davies.com
British, has lived in Sweden & Denmark

5. The contract is signed

It's official, the move is happening. I've told everyone, but now I'm having second thoughts. I keep thinking about what we'll miss out on here. It feels like too much is happening.

———

At some point the romance of living in a foreign country will seem, well, a little less romantic. But don't forget those initial feelings of falling in love with your dream.

This is the moment to take a few deep breaths, go for a walk, and reconnect with all the reasons you chose to take this path. Accept moving is a process and you're just getting started, so don't stress out about things that haven't even happened yet.

Stay in the present.

Preparing for change is ALWAYS hard, and something this big can feel overwhelming. It doesn't mean you should regret your decision or change your mind. *Would you have decided to quit giving birth when labor was at its most intense?* Of course not. You knew the best thing that ever happened to you was on its way. So stay strong. This decision is one of the best you've ever made, now you just have to see it through.

When moving gets intense, and everything is whirling through your head, it simply means change is coming. Every expat goes through this phase *no matter how many times they've moved.* Bear in mind any problem can be fixed – lost passports can be reissued, plane tickets rescheduled, medical records reprinted – there is no disaster so large that patience and fortitude can't find a solution.

OUR ADVICE
It's natural for you to worry with such a big change ahead. Take it step by step and everything will be fine.

'Doubt yourself and you doubt everything you see. Judge yourself and you see judges everywhere. But if you listen to the sound of your own voice, you can rise above doubt and judgment. And you can see forever.'

Nancy Lopez, Retired US Golfer

---

6. The kids don't want to go

The move is a week away and the kids are panicking.
They're clutching at straws to figure out ways to stay here.
I hate being the "mean parent," tearing them away from
friendships and a life they love. I wish I could promise
the move will be great, but I can't and that makes me
feel guilty.

————————

Kids are resistant to lots of things their parents want them to do, but don't get trapped in guilt. Sure you can't promise paradise, but you *can* promise them an adventure and the memory of a lifetime.

If they're not buying that... it's not too early to start planning your first vacation. Get them excited about a place they *do* want to go.

If they're worried about school and making friends ask the school in your new area if another student your kid's age can email them. Having a peer's opinion can go a long way to assuage worries. (The blessings of the Internet in a global world.)

Remember, we are all resistant to the unknown. It's easier to take the path more traveled, but keep reassuring them that when they arrive and start school, they're going to meet other kids going through the same thing they are experiencing. Their enthusiasm will wax and complaints will wane. It's all going to happen in time.

Don't let guilt cloud your advice. Keep listening, knowing that ultimately this experience will be for their growth. Overcoming challenges builds strength of character – a skill that will last a lifetime.

OUR ADVICE
As the move gets closer, resistance is normal. Hold their hand and keep listening. Don't let guilt cloud your parental voice of reason.

WORDS TO REMEMBER

'You can't make everyone happy.
You are not pizza.'

Anonymous

16

7. Where to live

Our family has always lived in the suburbs near the kids' school, but living in the burbs in our new country will make for a long commute to work and school is in a busy area. Most expats live near school, but I can't imagine life without a big back yard. How do I choose which area to live in?

_____

You might not know which area to live in, but you do know yourself. Are you the type of person who needs people? Do you enjoy being a core part of a group or do you feel more comfortable on the outside, stepping into a circle of friends when it suits you?

When moving to a new country we tend to look for the lifestyle that emulates the last place we were happy. If we lived in a house in the "burbs" we might associate happiness with a large dwelling place and yard. But before you make the house vs. high-rise decision, take a good honest look at yourself.

If you need people, live near your main source of socializing regardless of the type of housing available. If you have school-aged children it's a no brainer, stay close to the school or wherever most families live that will be the center of your community life. If you like your space or feel overwhelmed by groups then living a little further out is okay. If you're honest about who you are, you'll find the right home for you.

Happiness and success in your expat life has less to do with your type of housing and more to do with finding what suits you and your family's personality. We've seen unhappy expats because they held onto the big house in the country dream when what they needed was a small house near the school with an easy commute that offered more time to be involved. Know yourself and choose accordingly.

OUR ADVICE
Don't necessarily try to recreate what you had, look for the area that supports you and your family's social needs.

From those who have been there

An expat story

"As we were preparing to move abroad, the big question of where to live seemed a daunting decision to make considering I was not familiar with the city at all.

In order to narrow our options, my husband and I chose to pursue accommodations similar to what we call "home." I convinced myself we needed to create something familiar because I thought that would make our adjustment easier.

When we arrived we spent six weeks in a temporary apartment in the city, near the school, until our container arrived from the US. I walked the kids to school every day, we discovered beautiful parks, spent time making friends and discovered a whole new way of living.

Once our boxes arrived we moved into the house we chose in the suburbs. We had a yard, the kids had their trampoline and a lifestyle similar to what we had at home.

When we had unpacked and settled into our routine, it was obvious I had tried to recreate our living arrangements in a place, in a society, which is nothing like the place we knew as home. After a couple of months, I longed to be in the city.

I wanted to be closer to the school, closer to the social events and happenings, closer to the restaurants and bakeries, etc. It was then I realized I was missing out on an opportunity to experience something completely unique and new.

For our family, living in the city, in an apartment, would have been another part of the adventure.

I now understand it's not necessary to stick with what you know to find comfort and happiness, and embracing what the new host has to offer can make the adjustment easier."

Misty Wright – Creative Homemaker
American, lives in Sweden

8. The look-see

There's so much to do in so little time, I can't possibly choose a house that quickly. I have five different areas to explore – four homes to tour in each – plus three schools to visit. I need to set up a bank account, check mobile phone plans, and research local gyms and playgrounds. And I'm expected to meet the new boss's wife... all in five days!

We realize it seems like an overwhelming task, but you're not alone in sorting out all the details (even if you feel alone). If you've been allotted five days, experience will have told the company or relocation agency that it's time enough. If you can, let HR or your relocation agent put your schedule together. If not, take a deep breath and know that just like countless expats before you, it can be done. You will get there and make all the right decisions.

When moving into new territory you might feel inclined to take control and micromanage, but if you can, rely on the people who have been there before and use their advice. Recommendations from others will save you enormous amounts of time, money, and headaches. Ask for help – we can't emphasize this enough. Seek out information from those who have been through the process, it's invaluable.

If you're *really* feeling stressed, you might try extending your trip by a day or two. Or possibly your spouse can schedule a return "work trip" to take care of anything left undone. In most countries, if the move is happening in the spring or early summer, you'll still have time to scout around and find a place to live, but not always. Don't assume – sometimes rentals go fast, so let the local experts be your guides.

Of course, many expats won't get a "look-see" opportunity. When government or military staff is relocated it's usually without a prior visit. Housing is assigned or subject to "pools" of available contracts. But the aforementioned advice still applies, trust and rely on those who have gone before and don't hesitate to ask questions. Your best resources will be your fellow expats.

OUR ADVICE
Rely on your relocation agent and other expats. They have been through it before and can help you prioritize.

From those who have been there

An expat story

"In 2004 my husband was offered a job in Singapore. After seven years in Brussels, and two small children, it felt like a great opportunity.

The week we arrived in Singapore, it did not start well. My husband came down with a high fever and raging sore throat on arrival, which meant the school visits organized for the next day were a sleep-deprived, heavily-medicated emotional roller-coaster, especially when we found out there was a six month waiting list at our preferred school. We realized we'd have to research other options fast.

The search for suitable accommodation looked promising when the relocation agent picked us up on days two and three with an impressive spreadsheet of properties to visit. However, we soon found that with our budget this was going to be quite a challenge, as nothing seemed to come close to our expectations. With our hopes of easily securing schooling and somewhere to live evaporating, we met up with our friends (coincidentally also on a look-see trip), for a much-needed Singapore Sling or two in the Long Bar at Raffles Hotel.

They were in high spirits having settled on a school with available places. And their larger housing budget meant they found the perfect house complete with swimming pool. As we reported on our not so positive progress to date, I felt the lack of sleep, combined with a to-do list which seemed to be getting longer, overwhelm me and I burst into tears – not my proudest moment!

My friend suggested a little Montessori school she had discovered in her research, which turned out to be a great place for the girls to start until places came available at our preferred school. We didn't find suitable accommodation on our look-see trip, so stayed in a serviced apartment for a few weeks after relocating, during which time we found a fabulous place that had just come on the market to rent.

The whole experience taught me that things don't always go to plan however organized you are, but that's fine and often you end up in a better situation as a result. Use your contacts and their experiences as well as the company's support and advice. Finally, it is sometimes easier to sort some things out once you have relocated, so don't panic if you haven't finalised everything during a look-see trip."

Alexa Servante – Portfolio Wife
British, has lived in Belgium, Singapore, Germany & South Africa

9. The house hunt

The houses in my host country are vastly different from anything I've ever experienced before. They aren't to my taste and I can't imagine how my furniture will look inside them. If I can't picture myself there, how do I make a choice?

Some people live in the weirdest places, *or so it seems.* The contrast might feel jolting to what feels "normal." The building, the interiors, the layouts and neighborhood could have a very foreign feel… because they *are foreign.*

One of the upsides about living abroad is you can try out a totally new living situation, knowing it won't be forever. Instead of searching for what you're accustomed to with a home, we recommend you search for a home that fits the lifestyle you want to create.

Do you plan to travel a lot and want a home that's easy to maintain? Then see what it's like to live in an apartment. Have you always wanted a living space with room to entertain? How about a life without yard work on the weekends? Would a fireplace and large picture window feel cozy? Knock yourself out!

Here's your chance to try something different. Have a good think about what you want out of life and see this as an opportunity.

In the "right here and now," when you just want a place, hunting for the right one feels like an enormous hassle, but remain patient and persistent and you'll be glad you did. The perfect house is out there, one that will bring you and your family a lot of enjoyment.

Just because you can't picture yourself in a house with large ceiling fans, doesn't mean you won't be grateful to have them when the hot muggy season hits. The housing features that might seem weird at first, likely represent something inherent to living there that you don't quite understand yet.

OUR ADVICE
Look for the house that offers you the lifestyle you want, even if it feels foreign to begin with. It will become your home because it will be your home.

An expat story

"We moved from Belgium to Singapore in 2005. When we went house hunting we saw a bunch of condos, but we couldn't fathom the idea of ourselves living there, and the houses we saw seemed surreal. They were cold tile or extravagant marble, neither of which gave me a warm fuzzy feeling, with ceiling fans that were old fashioned or out of place. It was hard to get my head around it.

We didn't get a house on that trip – my husband chose our house on a subsequent trip and sent pictures. I was hopeful, because he seemed to really like it. He said he chose it for the lifestyle it would give us. When we arrived in Singapore, he brought me there and it took all my willpower not to break down and cry. My first impression was awful! I couldn't imagine us living there. It felt like a tacky holiday home with bright red walls and it was just... I don't know, weird. As soon as I was alone I sobbed and called the one friend I knew. She tried to comfort me, but I wasn't having it.

But when I moved in, I was amazed. It was always hot there, so I loved having the cool tile floors. The ceiling fans were a true godsend and, actually, we spent eighty percent of our family time on the large covered terrace that was at the heart of the house. It was PERFECT.

I am so grateful my husband made the choice he did, because to be honest, I couldn't have done it myself."

Stefanie Blackstone – Traveling Family Pillar
Belgian, has lived in Italy, Singapore, Japan & Sweden

10. Organizing the house for the move

I'm wandering from room to room, trying to figure out how to prepare for the upcoming move. The sheer amount of things to organize, donate, and get rid of feels paralyzing. Where do I begin?

―――――――

We don't mean to alarm you, but getting everything *into* the boxes is not the big deal, it's taking it all out again at the other end. In fact, you can leave part one to your packers. That's what they are paid for, right?

Instead, focus your attention on taking the time to say goodbye, spending that extra hour with your grandparents or going on one last girls' night out before you leave. Those are the moments you will cherish most when you need a boost on the other side.

If you desperately want to go through things, get rid of clothes, and generally get your thoughts together on the subject. But don't do it to the detriment of enjoying those last few weeks with friends and family.

The bottom line is that no matter how much you sort and purge before you move, there will be a whole lot more of it when you get to the other side. When you're unpacking, you'll want to take that time because you'll be creating your home there as well.

So for now, conserve your emotional and physical energies for the unexpected events that will surely pop up and leave the real organizing for when you get there. Most countries have a donation box.

OUR ADVICE
Don't do more than you need to. Prioritize the time you have with your friends and family first.

WORDS TO REMEMBER

'People are more important than things.'

**Randy Pausch, American Professor
at Carnegie Mellon University**

---

11. Take it or store it?

I love my golf clubs, but I doubt I'll find a green in Greenland. Do I put them in storage? What about all the other things I don't think I'll need? Do I leave them behind?

The short answer is "no."

Don't leave what you love behind. Take what you cherish. It's better to have what you love and use it if the opportunity arises than to spend two years missing out on your favorite activity or enjoying your favorite decorations.

When you put things in storage what you're really saying is this isn't important to me or doesn't belong in my life right now. If there are items you don't need or use, go ahead and leave them behind (or get rid of them), but don't pack away your favorite things just because you're uncertain you'll find a way to use them.

If space restrictions are an issue then realistically select what is most important to you. But remember, if it's something you love, you'll continue to love it no matter where you are in the world.

Greenland boasts the World's Ice Golf Championship in Uummannaq every spring. You'll definitely need your clubs there. The point is, you don't want to miss out on what makes living abroad interesting – doing what you love in a new way. Sure it might be the same game, but being an expat means you play the "old" game with new rules. It's part of the adventure.

OUR ADVICE
Don't overuse storage. If you can miss it for a couple of years, you can probably miss it forever... and if you love it, don't leave it behind.

Take it or leave it?

To help decide what to keep and what to let go of, ask yourself these questions.

If the answer is "No", let it go.

1. Do I love it?

2. Do I need it?

3. Does it support who I am in my life now?

4. Does it make me smile?

5. Do I associate positive memories or emotions with it?

6. If it needs to be fixed or repaired, am I willing to do so before I leave?

12. Weight limits

We have more stuff than our weight limit allows. I can store some things, but we need to reduce our overall weight. Do I get rid of the baby crib when we still might want to have another? I have bookcases that may or may not fit in our new home and books are SO heavy, but they're books I love. Where do I start?

—————————

Start by taking a good hard look around and see that although a lot of memories are attached to what you see, if you leave things behind and end up needing them, they can be replaced.

It's not so much about the stuff, it's about the associations you have with them. The trampoline you saw your kids jump on throughout the years and the piano your kids learned to play on can be hard to let go. But remember you are about to embark on a whole new adventure that right now you can't imagine. Your new country will come with new experiences and shedding some of the weight beforehand will create space for new memories later.

If weight limits allow, take all the things you love and figure out what you'll do with them once you get there. If not, let it go. Think of it as a chance to practice a key expat skill – being creative at "making do."

If you're worried about your books, buy a Kindle. If you don't take that baby crib and the stork makes an appearance, expats are great at setting up social media groups for buying, selling or giving items away, so baby is sure to find a soft comfy place to lie its head.

Yes, it would be wonderful if you could keep everything that's meaningful to you, but if you had everything you needed, there'd be no reason to go out and explore to find unexpected treasures to add to your memories.

OUR ADVICE
Remember, just because you're getting rid of some of your stuff doesn't mean you'll lose your memories.

Where to begin

Preparing for the move

Things to remember that experience has taught us:

1. **Check the local customs laws in your new country.**
   Be aware that some countries confiscate your shipment if it contains banned items.

2. **Pre-organize empty box pick-up for after you've unpacked.**
   The movers will do most of the unboxing, but there will always be boxes you want to unpack yourself. Agree with the company ahead of time that there will be a "box pickup" after you've emptied all your things.

3. **Empty your trashcans.**
   Or you might be unpacking smelly garbage at the other end.

4. **Ship copies of your passports, medical reports, and other valuable papers.**
   Take originals with you when you travel, but keep a copy in the shipment for back up.

5. **Ship extra medications that you use regularly.**
   Most countries have an equivalent of what you use, but it might take a while to find it.

6. **Ship favorite cereals and snacks.**
   You'll find new favorites in your host country, but old favorites are a nice treat.

13. I'm leaving, shouldn't I be sad?

I'm saying goodbye, but it doesn't feel like goodbye. I'm not even crying. It doesn't feel real yet. I'm focused on logistics and getting things ready for the move and I don't know how to act sometimes.

———————

Maybe you're not sad because right now you are exactly where you need to be, preparing for your journey ahead. Your mind is filled with logistics, excitement, curiosity and decision-making beyond your wildest imagination.

You're busy... you've got lots of things to do, and saying goodbye might not feel like one of them. If that's the case, it could be because you can't cope with that right now. *You need a fair amount of denial to get through the initial work of moving.*

Hug your friends anyway, go out to dinner with them, make time for the rituals of goodbye so when the haze of denial lifts you'll have lots of good memories to look back on. If it doesn't feel real yet, that's okay. Each of us deals with this process differently and, to be honest, each move is different too.

The reality of saying goodbye might hit you when you're on the way to the airport or after you get off the plane.

Eventually emotions will surface, but for now there's so much to do, saying goodbye might feel surreal.

OUR ADVICE
There is no right way to feel. Just make sure you take time to say goodbye to your friends so you won't regret it later.

'What I think is not necessarily what I feel, and what I feel is not necessarily, what I think.'

Santosh Kalwar, Nepalese writer

---

14. Feeling a mess

We're leaving tomorrow and I can't stop crying. I'm a mess! I need to be strong for my family but I just can't. I'm worried if I fall apart, who will keep it together?

You are who you are and feel what you feel. You can't deny how you're feeling and covering it up won't work – *not for long anyway.* Embarking on the expat journey involves your entire family, it's a group effort and tears of a mysterious origin are par for the course. At some point each family member will have a moment requiring support to get them through. Right now the moment is yours.

You can cry and still be strong. You can be excited and sad at the same time. Tears are indicators that it's time to talk to the family in a different way about the move. Assure them emotional turmoil is normal and they all might go through it. You going first could be just what they need, so share this with them.

If it all becomes too much give yourself some space. In one of your lucid moments, make a list. Ask for help from your partner, kids and friends. They'll feel needed and reassured that when it's their turn you'll be there to support them too.

As for keeping it together?

It will come together. Like so many things in life, all the preparation you did before you fell apart will prove its worth... and the things that fall through the cracks can either be fixed later, or they weren't worth the trouble to begin with. You've got this.

OUR ADVICE
Between the tears, make a list and outsource some stuff to your partner, kids or friends.

Where to begin

Packing for your air shipment

It can be helpful to send a few boxes ahead by air to be there when you arrive. Check if your temporary accommodation will be furnished or not. Either way, here are some things to think about for your initial shipment.

Kitchen items
Large/paring and bread knife
Baking sheet and pan
Large pot and frying pan
Pyrex baking dish
Can opener/bottle opener

Scissors
Peeler/grater
Colander
Measuring cups and spoons
Utensils
Glassware/plates/bowls
Large serving bowl and mixing bowls
Storage/lunch containers
Spatula/serving spoon/slotted spoon
Table cloth
Salt/pepper/spices
Favorite tea and coffee

Bedding and towels
Set of sheets with blanket/personal
Pillows
Set of towels per person
Extra towels for beach or pool

Office and school supplies
Notebook
Pens and pencils
Permanent waterproof marker
Scotch tape
Glue stick
Duct tape
Reference books
Children's books
Reading material for school or entertainment

Things that are also helpful
Laundry baskets
Hand sanitizer
Wet wipes
Small packets of Kleenex
First aid kit
Games and toys to entertain kids
A few gift items unique to your country
to offer as gifts
Camera or video equipment
Portable speaker
Digital TV system, i.e., Apple TV or Kindle
Videogame system and games

15. Moving day

*It's moving day (sigh). My husband's working, my
daughter's Snapchatting, my son's playing football and
I'm freaking out. Everything is getting packed but they're
all acting like nothing is happening. Is it normal that
we're not coming together on this?*

_____

Watching your life being reduced to a few hundred boxes
can make you feel very small in a big universe. For some
people it's freeing and for others it's frightening. This is a
big thing and, quite frankly, there's no "normal" reaction.

As much as you'd like your family to stand as a unit
everyone will process the transition differently. Some
will want to celebrate the moment and others will want
to take a nap. Their emotions will indicate what they
need, so go with it.

You're still in this together even if everyone is dealing
with the move in their own way. Be patient with yourself
and others. There are worse things they could be doing
than playing sports or texting friends. Whatever is going
on, it's temporary.

OUR ADVICE
**Each family member will deal with the move
the best way they know how. Go with the flow.**

Packing for the plane

Things to keep front and center in your carry on:

1. Medications

2. Passports

3. Medical records/vaccine records

4. Educational transcripts

5. Special jewelry

6. Deeds to your home

7. Birth certificates, marriage certificate, social security cards

Part II
On the Move

1. Getting off the plane

We just stepped foot in our new host country – it's SO different. We've read the guidebooks, but, as a family, how do we begin to soak it all up?

Everyone absorbs stimuli differently. While one of you is ready to explore, another wants to find a comfortable place to sit. Immersing yourself in a new environment is an emotional experience for both the individual and the family as a whole.

Monitor how family members are doing by playing a game: "I Spy for expats." Only in this version everyone points out stuff they notice – whatever catches their eye – and says it out loud. It'll get the family talking and, if you listen carefully, you'll learn some important things.

You'll see that some family members are noticing what's familiar in this new strange environment, while others are attracted to what's different and unusual. Those who search for the familiar might be looking for points of reference to feel at home – their comfort zone – while those searching for the newness have a need to explore what's unique before they can find their place.

Striking a balance within the family is a delicate matter. Listening to what interests each individual will help you understand why one might resist the adjustment and another embraces the newness of it all.

OUR ADVICE
Make it a game, point out what's different and what's familiar to get a glimpse of how each family member will come to terms with their new home.

An expat story

This is a Facebook post from a fellow expat upon arrival in China. She is quoting Alan Cohen, author:

"...'It takes a lot of courage to release the familiar and seemingly secure, to embrace the new. But there is no real security in what is no longer meaningful. There is more security in the adventurous and exciting, for in movement there is life, and in change there is power.'

Here we go again... we wait for you in Beijing! Love, Sole."

Soledad Matteozzi – Patagonian World Traveler
Argentinian has lived in Sweden & China

2. Reality hits and it's overwhelming

This was supposed to be an exciting adventure, yet it feels more like one big ball of frustration. The language makes no sense, neither does the money. The street signs, maps and stores are all confusing. It's going to take a miracle to find milk! This wasn't the adventure I'd planned.

———————

It can be hard to keep seeing your life as an adventure when you're standing in a tunnel unable to see the light at the end. When excitement turns into frustration your positive attitude can turn skeptical, maybe even fearful.

It's called "expat overload" and it happens to the best of us.

Have you ever watched people on a roller coaster? Some have smiles on their faces, while others look as though they're staring death in the face. They both paid good money to ride the rides so why do they have such different reactions?

Because fear and excitement are opposites of the same emotion, they represent a negative or positive interpretation of the same stimuli. Does knowing that help you right now? Not really, but next time you're feeling fearful remind yourself that you can look at your situation differently.

Life is like a roller coaster no matter where you are in the world. You can either flip your fear and enjoy the ride or wait it out, knowing the ride will be over soon.

OUR ADVICE
Fear and frustration will turn back into excitement again soon. In the meantime, feeling overwhelmed is completely justifiable and it will pass.

WORDS TO REMEMBER

'Did you know that fear and excitement show up the same way in your body? If you were hooked up to a machine that monitored your response to fear or to excitement, your body would respond the same way to both experiences. That means the body can't tell the difference between the two...

So, today, choose excitement over fear. Choose awe over terror or nervousness. Move forward instead of staying stuck. Or, when you feel afraid, rename the emotion; simply call your fear "excitement" or "awe" and see if the way you feel doesn't change along with the new name.'

Nina Amir, Creation Coach, Author and Speaker

3. Feeling lost in your new world

All my old routines have vanished or have no place in this new world where I am living. I have no idea how to organize my day. I have to-do lists, but even that feels unmanageable. I don't know where to start.

———————

Welcome to your new world where *anything* is possible. The journey starts now. All that packing, planning, and moving... that was *preliminary stuff*. It's time to get down to the business of living, which means sorting out what you're going to do each day.

Begin with building new routines that make sense in the world you've landed in. Make habits a part of each day so you have anchors to your daily routine to support you. Habits will help you feel comfortable, confident, and more at home.

Read the morning newspaper online, brew your favorite cup of Joe (even if you import it from home), pray, eat dinner as a family, go to the gym, empty your dishwasher each morning. Whatever helps you feel centered, do it.

Building a few simple routines into your day will ground you so the chaos of the unknowns won't distract you from accomplishing your goals. Creating some predictability will give you a sense of flow and purpose.

OUR ADVICE
When your whole life has changed, build
structure into your new world by creating
routines, habits and rituals for yourself.
Start with one and build from there.

WORDS TO REMEMBER

'We are what we repeatedly do.
Excellence then is not an act,
but a habit.'

Aristotle, Greek Philosopher & Scientist

---

4. Family and friends don't understand

When I talk to my friends back home about what's going on in my life, they just kind of nod and change the subject. They don't understand and I feel like I might be losing them.

It's hard when you've always talked openly with your friends and all of a sudden, conversations feel distant. Try putting yourself in their position. Could you have understood your host country before actually living there?

They can't relate to your new world, but it doesn't mean they don't care or don't miss you.

Life as an expat is full of privileges and experiences your friends back home can't fathom. You're employing domestic help, complaining about buying margarine, eating strange foods, figuring out new customs – doing things you can't fully explain in a Skype chat. Your friends care and they want to understand, it's just beyond their scope of reality.

They'll always love you, but your worlds are growing apart. And that's okay.

Your hearts are still connected. These are friends who will be there for the Big Stuff. And when you see these friends again, face-to-face, you'll feel the same sense of love and caring you always did.

You never lose true friendships – they span continents, distance, space and time. In the meantime, talk to other expats who understand what you're going through and can support you in the here and now.

OUR ADVICE
Family and friends still love you, but don't expect them to understand. They simply can't. It doesn't mean they won't be there when the going gets tough.

WORDS TO REMEMBER

'Good friends are like stars, you don't always see them, but you know they are there.'

Christy Evans, (pseudonym of Christina F. York) American Author

---

5. The boxes can wait

I was invited to lunch with a group of moms after the first information session at school, but my boxes arrived yesterday so I declined and went home to unpack instead. Did I do the right thing?

———————

The short answer is no, but don't feel bad, you're learning.

During the first couple of months in your new country, prioritize socializing first and getting things "done" later. That may sound counter-intuitive, as if we're telling you to be lazy, but it's actually *more* work. Making new friends requires dedication, particularly in the beginning.

The first weeks of any school year offers gatherings and activities that might not come around later. They're crucial times because it's when all the 'newbies' come together looking for support and the veterans are there, happy and prepared to point the way.

While it's important to set up and establish your home, taking an extra day to get the boxes unpacked won't affect your long-term happiness, but laying the groundwork for establishing solid friendships will.

Don't put off joining a club or going to a PTA meeting or out to lunch with a new prospective friend, even if it's not your "thing." These activities will provide you with a sense of home and a support network to help navigate this new place. These friends will understand what you're going through and have oodles of useful information about things that interest you.

OUR ADVICE
The first few months in your expat life are key when it comes to meeting friends and building a support network. Don't let opportunities slip by because you're prioritizing practicalities.

WORDS TO REMEMBER

'Practical! On Wednesday afternoons
I could be practically anything!'

Kit Williams, British Artist, Illustrator & Author

---

6. Crying for no reason

 I feel happy. I'm getting settled, making new friends and I love our new home. I'm unpacked and new routines are falling into place. So why do I burst into tears for seemingly no reason at all?

It isn't unusual to feel teary and sad, even when things are going well. In fact, if you surveyed a crowd of expats you'd be surprised at how many have felt emotional instability. Remember, you've embarked on a great new life, but you're also grieving the loss of your old life – *even if you were happy to leave it behind.*

Change affects each of us differently. Your psyche is trying to keep up but you're asking a lot of it right now. If you're feeling well, but you're crying at odd times, the best thing to do is just let it happen.

Spending time and energy trying to figure out *why* you're sad will lead to finding reasons to be sad. And when you dwell on those reasons, you'll create more. It's a vicious circle and we strongly recommend you don't go there.

Acknowledge you're going through a lot, and probably taking on the rest of the family's emotions as well, so don't sweat it. A few tears can bring an abundance of relief and give you the space to go on enjoying life.

OUR ADVICE
You're in a grieving process. Don't try to understand the tears, allow them to flow knowing they are an intrinsic part of the process.

'But a mermaid has no tears, and therefore she suffers so much more.'

The Little Mermaid, Hans Christian Andersen

---

7. Exploring your new country

I want to start exploring, after all, that's why we came on this journey. But I'm not an experienced traveler. What savvy tips and tricks do I need to know before I plan a proper excursion?

———————

According to the *The Merriam Webster Dictionary*, an excursion is "a short trip especially for pleasure." A short trip can mean anything from going to the mall or spending a day or two hiking in the mountains. Who cares whether it's a "legitimate" exploratory adventure. Everything is an adventure to a new expat. Stepping out of your front door, engaging with the world in front of you, is an excursion of one kind or another.

Begin small and realize life is already an exploration. What do you think is fun? Do you like camping or skiing or scuba diving? Does your country offer an opportunity to try something you've never tried before? Say, paddle boarding or visiting pandas or exploring an excavation site?

Creating a memorable excursion only requires a willingness to follow a map and make a few wrong turns. It could be handy to bring along a few water bottles, a small stash of hidden bills, your insurance card and medication for two days longer than you think you'll need – should you be having so much fun you decide to stay longer.

If you want more travel tips ask around, most everyone is willing to offer up a travelogue. You can also find resources online and in local bookstores. But ultimately the best trips are the ones left open to chance. It's the things you don't plan that are often the highlights of the journey.

If you have the attitude that life is an excursion, then you'll take meaning from each new encounter. Your forays into a new part of town or shop or café are excursions in and of themselves. Take pleasure in discovery and as your confidence grows, so will your ability to venture further afield.

OUR ADVICE
There are no rules to exploring. Excursions will be all around you, just dive in.

WORDS TO REMEMBER

'Doubt increases with inaction.
Clarity reveals itself in momentum.
Growth comes from progress.
For all these reasons, BEGIN.'

Brendon Burchard, US High Performance Coach & Personal Development Trainer

8. Adapting to new currency

The new money system has me totally confused. I can't tell if I'm saving or overspending. At this rate, we'll never be able to afford a vacation.

_____

If you've ever played Monopoly then you know how easy it is to go from a wad of purple fifties to bust. It's "funny" money. It doesn't feel real because it isn't.

It's the same sort of thing when you're holding foreign currency – it's weird, like Monopoly money. Even though it's cold hard cash, in the beginning it doesn't feel that way.

Welcome to the wonderful world of exchange rates, cost of living differences, and shopping with a calculator. Figuring out prices and budgets can be maddening.

The reality is you'll make a few blunders. Either you don't have time to find a bargain, because you need it NOW, or what you need isn't readily available in the host country so you stock up. And sometimes you just have a good old-fashioned brain spasm and miscalculate.

At some point you'll spend more than you planned, so in the beginning add a line to your household budget called "expat educational costs," because learning to dispense your new funds requires practice.

With a bit of time, patience, and research you'll know exactly where to buy your favorites at a reasonable price and will get the hang of the cost of things. Be wise and sensible, but don't overstress about spending more than you'd planned. Those educational costs also pay for some great memories.

OUR ADVICE
While spending your new currency, you'll make mistakes. Enjoy the occasional splurge and mark it down to the cost of learning.

From those who have been there

An expat story

"When we moved to Tokyo my daughter was four. Leather goods cost a fortune there, so when I got a tip on reasonably priced, sensible shoes for toddlers, I jumped on it.

Off I went with her to the sales section of the department store where we found great shoes for a price that was still too expensive coming from Singapore, but very reasonable in my new world.

To celebrate we stopped at a little sushi restaurant to have lunch. My daughter LOVES sushi, so we had a heyday. It was our first sushi lunch since living there. The sushi chef was great and so attentive to my daughter; we were just soaking up our new world and loving it.

We were finally ready to go after an amazing afternoon, so I asked for the bill. To my shock, I had just spent over $250US on a lunch with my toddler! As exorbitant as it was, looking back I wouldn't trade that experience for anything. My daughter and I will remember it always."

Stefanie Blackstone – Traveling Family Pillar
Belgian, has lived in Italy, Singapore, Japan & Sweden

9. Not coping well

There is SO much to do to get settled in and it's all so confusing. Why is everything going wrong? I want to crawl under the covers and hide.

———————

With so much going on, the LAST thing you want to hear is, "Take a break." But when total frustration has you down... STOP. Stop everything. Rest. Give yourself permission to say HALT. *Arresto!*

It can feel like getting things done is what's keeping you upright and that everything will fall apart if you stop, but the truth is just about everything you have to do can wait a day or even a few. There's rarely a true emergency.

Distract yourself for a bit. Denial can be a really good place to live, *for a little while anyway.* A pause in your state of forward momentum will allow worries to take on a more realistic perspective and give you a chance to ground yourself again.

Spend the day watching television, read a book or go out for some retail therapy. Do whatever you do when you want to escape. Taking a break to regroup and find yourself again will actually give you the energy to tackle your projects and get things done faster and more efficiently.

Get some zzzzz's. After a good night's sleep, you'll wake up and discover the world is still turning and you'll be ready to take on the day.

OUR ADVICE
Give yourself a day off in denial and tomorrow will look a whole lot better.

Where to begin

Feeling overwhelmed?

Based on 'The Overwhelmed Cheat Sheet' from *The Simplified Planner* by Emily Ley:

1. Declutter

2. Sort it out and organize

3. Put things where you use them

4. Get it out, write it down

5. Prioritize

6. Make it happen

7. Decide what matters

8. Say YES to the important stuff

9. Say NO to the rest

10. Aversion to big gatherings

I get so nervous when I go to large gatherings and coffee mornings. I know I have to go to understand the community better, but I feel so awkward. I don't know what to say to people. Small talk isn't my forte.

If you're uncomfortable in a room full of strangers, you're not alone. Big gatherings are anxiety producing for a lot of people. You might even feel it's easier to be lonely than face your social fears.

If you're anxious, keep in mind that everyone else is anxious too. They may appear to be comfortable now, but at some point they were new like you, moving with their families from across the world, feeling like "strangers."

At expat gatherings it's safe to assume you have one huge thing in common – none of you are from here. That gives you the perfect "go-to" question to start a conversation:

"Where are you from?" (said in a falsely confident, but nonetheless genuine tone).

Back home this question might have resulted in a single sentence, but in THIS world you've just opened a whole host of topics.

At your next gathering, make it a goal to talk to two people using your newfound friends: "Where are you from?" and "How did you get here?" Even if you're feeling uncomfortable, say hello, exchange email addresses or Facebook names. A few conversations in and you'll find people are a lot like you. But you have to meet them first.

OUR ADVICE
Attend social gatherings to get the valuable information you need. It's easier than you think to start a conversation in this world. Simply ask how someone got here and you're set.

WORDS TO REMEMBER

'Call it a clan, call it a network, call it a tribe, call it a family: whatever you call it, whoever you are, you need one.'

Families, Jane Howard, US Journalist, Author & Editor

---

11. Making a house your home

This is a temporary assignment, but my kids don't like the paint in their room and I'm itching to plant a flowerbed in our garden. Should I do it? I mean, I'm only going to be here a little while.

_____

When your contract is only for a year or two, you might think investing in such a short-term project is a waste of time and money. Why put energy into a place that's only temporary, right? The answer is because if you do, you can enjoy it *now.*

Now is what you've got. Now is where you're living.

Don't postpone happiness or enjoyment. Life is too short to put up with things you don't like. Or said another way, life is too loooong to do things you don't like. Either way you look at it, all you have is the present moment, so make the most of it.

In the expat world, two years is LONG! Just think... if you paint, there's no worrying that five years from now you won't like the color, or your two-year-old will be tired of her room when she's ten. *Isn't that a good thing?*

If you spend this fabulous opportunity only living halfway, you'll turn the deeper experiences of expat life into uncertainty for you and your family. Don't put yourself through the unhappiness of living in a place you haven't made your own for two whole years, because who knows, two years could turn into three, then four. So paint the walls, pull the weeds, and get to know the neighbors. This is your home, right here, right now. Make the most of it!

OUR ADVICE
In the expat world "now" is all you've got. Make the most of it with your heart and soul to make it your home.

WORDS TO REMEMBER

'If not now, when?'

Hillel the Elder (110BC – 10AD), Jewish Religious Leader

---

12. Feeling anxious in your new life

The thought of going out to do things makes me feel anxious. I never used to have a problem shopping or talking to strangers, but now I act like a shy five-year-old. I want to be confident, but I don't feel it.

———————

They say, "Forty is the new thirty." In the expat world read, "Different is the new normal." As an expat you'll encounter thousands of unfamiliar situations – it's normal to feel out of place or anxious... *at first*. In the beginning *everything* feels daunting, no matter how civilized your host country is. This vulnerable, unsure feeling you have is inevitable, but it won't last and there are things you can do to feel more confident.

Start by developing some routines in your life to ground you – habits not only make you more productive, they give you confidence. Ask fellow expats for help. Ask someone to take you to the grocery store and explain how it works. A more seasoned expat can save you time and build your confidence with their experience. And nothing is more reassuring than sitting down with a fellow expat, listening as they answer the question, "What was your first three months like?"

Everyone goes through an adjustment period, your "new normal." Be observant with an open mind, keep a childlike perspective of wonder and curiosity. Above all, don't berate yourself if you make a mistake – learn and move on, you'll find your footing.

OUR ADVICE
In the beginning it can be daunting, but stick with it. Soon "different" will become the new "normal."

From those who have been there

An expat story

"Before moving to Stockholm, I lived within a seven-mile radius of my childhood home my entire life. I was now in a new and unfamiliar frontier on many levels: the real world outside my door, the spaces that filled my thoughts, my feelings, and the physical walls indoors I would now call home. Everything felt irreparably broken, displaced and empty.

When we arrived the city was quiet. I didn't know it then, but Stockholmers go to their summer cottages from early July until mid-August. I felt the desperate need to fill the empty, echoing apartment with the comfort and familiar smell of my Puerto Rican cooking, but I froze at the supermarket, unable to comprehend the labels, the towering prices (could milk really cost that much?) and the unspoken rules for navigating through a shared space in a country where breaking cultural rules is a serious social blunder. I left the store in tears, upset with myself for feeling so narrow-minded and inexperienced. For the next six weeks we ate the same simple dinner of roasted chicken and vegetables with rice, as I struggled to learn my way through the market and overcome the sinking feeling we had made a mistake leaving everything we knew to be familiar and true.

Soon after, school started and new routines began to form. In those early days, a kind woman asked how things were going. Much to my surprise, that thoughtful question opened the bursting floodgates and a stream of tears ran down my face as I released everything I'd held back since arriving on that sunny day in July – the anxiety, fear, sadness and confusion of leaving everything behind. With the understanding only another expat can offer, she looked at me and said, "You know what you need? Fika!" (Fika is a sweet Swedish tradition of a shared coffee or tea and pastries over intimate conversation.) "Tomorrow morning we will have fika together and everything will be fine."

Of course she was right. Fika with friends makes everything better."

Nancy Johnson – Mom and co-creator of The Latina A.R.M.Y.
Puerto Rican, has lived in the US & Sweden

13. Not feeling yourself

I'm not usually like this; I have no desire to do all the things I used to. I was active and energetic back home, but right now I don't recognize myself. I want to get my groove back, but how?

If you're feeling lost within yourself, passing time surfing the Internet, reading mindless magazines or pouring yourself a glass of wine before noon, you're still in what we call the "transition phase." It might surprise you how totally unlike your usual self that can be.

We have seen the mightiest of women succumb to the Xbox, daytime television and obsessive cleaning during the transition phase, only to come out the other side stronger, better and happier.

What you need to know is this – the transition phase is a bridge from your former self to the self you're still trying to figure out. Your world just got a whole lot BIGGER. Life has changed drastically. Your eyes are now open to a gazillion different ways of being. It's too much to take in all at once. It may feel like you're a puzzle piece and you need to set yourself outside of the box, until you can see the big picture and figure out where you belong. Finding "your reality" takes time. To cope, you might go a little off kilter. But not to worry, you'll find your way to the other side.

Go to events nonetheless – make contact with actual human beings and before you know it, you'll find outlets and enterprises that will help you to feel like yourself again. A different, new, slightly altered self, but nonetheless... yourself.

OUR ADVICE
It's a phase. This is a big deal and sometimes you need to take time to regroup before you find balance.

Where to begin

Ways to look for your groove

A list to inspire out-of-the box thinking in your new country.

1. Call someone you just met and invite them to lunch

2. Learn how to belly dance

3. Start your own travel blog

4. Find your Church

5. Keep a photo journal

6. Play on the Xbox

7. Visit an art museum

8. Discover the joys of Indian cooking

9. Watercolor

10. Read the classics

11. Create a scavenger hunt for your kids

12. Find antiques at local markets

13. Check the local papers for events in your area

14. Host a dinner party

15. Make something to decorate your home

16. Build something with Legos

17. Find yourself through interpretive dance

18. Be a dog walker

19. Go to the nearest amusement park for the day

20. Shop for a "conversation" piece for your living room

14. Missing home

I miss home a lot more than I thought I would. When I go outside here, the sights and faces... everything is so unfamiliar. I want the comfort and ease of home.

——————

Homesickness happens to everyone at different times during the expat transition. Doubts and sadness arise from missing your comfort zone and the people you loved and relied on in times of change. Nothing can replace what you had back home.

But when you stop looking back, you can begin to create a new comfort zone and new friends who will support you in this quirky, crazy world we call *expat life*. This is the time to step back and remember all the great reasons why you chose to be an expat. The world is opening up to you. You are experiencing new things and gaining new insights. Your children are learning new languages and understanding the world in a whole new way. How exciting!

You're exactly where you need to be right now. Just because it feels hard, doesn't mean it's not right. You're allowed to miss your friends, your family and your familiar surroundings, but don't dwell. Stay present to all the great things happening around you.

Keep looking forward, embrace this new experience and you'll find a second set of friends and a new perspective on family. Your world will expand before your very eyes.

OUR ADVICE
The bigger your comfort zone becomes here, the more your longing for home will diminish.

WORDS TO REMEMBER

'Don't look back;
you're not going that way.'

Anonymous

---

15. When does it get easier?

I really want to start enjoying life but everything still feels hard. It's like I'm on a roller coaster that doesn't let up. When will it get easier?

So you've learned to convert money and know where to buy ketchup and take your dry cleaning – that's a great start. When you're three months into your move and you're still not completely unpacked *and can't even order a beer in the local language yet, don't dismay.*

Settling in takes time. There's a lot to navigate – different money, culture, values, food, customs, language, stores, schools, not to mention making new friends and the emotional turmoil you and your family have gone through. Whew!

Before you think there's something wrong, look again with a wider view and notice what's *right*. Notice all the progress you've made. You're doing just fine. Pat yourself on the back. Be impressed!

We'd love to give you a firm hard rule and say it takes six months until you begin to feel settled in, but sometimes it takes longer. You're absorbing an awful lot and doing a ton of adapting and improvising – be patient with yourself and this process.

When you least expect it something will just click. You'll have friends and events in your diary, and your life and routine will fall into place. If it's not fun yet, hang in there, it will be.

OUR ADVICE
The first six months are usually the toughest, but don't give up. In time it will feel like second nature.

From those who have been there

An expat story

"In September 2014, my husband asked me out of the blue, "What do you think about relocating to Stockholm? Oh, and I'm talking about next month!"

To be honest I didn't want to move, after seven years outside of Israel in Atlanta USA, and London, UK. All I wanted was to stay home in Israel. We had just bought a house the year before, the kids were settled in school and family was close – why move again? And of all the places in the world to frozen Stockholm?

A month later we arrived in Stockholm to one of the darkest Novembers ever. I didn't know anybody – everybody ran away before and after school, nobody talked to me, no playdates, no friends and no wi-fi, television or furniture in the house (it took eight weeks for the container to arrive).

I so badly wanted to go back home, it was a disaster, worst ever. To top it off, everybody was preparing to disappear for a month for Christmas so the timing of our arrival couldn't have been worse.

After the winter break, some ladies I didn't know were collecting money to join a fitness class for a fund-raiser run by the school, taking place the last week of January.

I joined the class and met some lovely ladies and, after the event, one of the moms in my youngest son's class asked if I wanted to continue with a weekly workout she was doing.

I joined and met more people who told me there were actually clubs! From November until the end of April I hadn't known there were clubs. I joined the Friday Walking Club and met more parents.

By the end of the school year in June, my whole family agreed that although the beginning was horrible, this was by far our best relocation yet."

Yael Shoham – Starbucks VIP
Israeli, has lived in the US, UK & Sweden

16. It seems so easy for everyone else

All the other newbies seem to have this place decoded while I'm still struggling. Am I missing something, or am I just not good at this?

––––––––

We can't emphasize enough – **talking to other expats is key**. No matter how big the smile or how seemingly effortless the transition is for someone else, we can pretty much guarantee they're going through (or have gone through) the same feelings you have, to a greater or lesser extent. So talk to them!

The minute you start comparing yourself to others, you start down a slippery slope. It's easy to forget a lot can hide behind a smiling face. Making assumptions can be very misleading.

Some expats seem to cope with aspects that overwhelm you, while others struggle in areas you take for granted but we ALL experience a range of emotional turmoil in our own unique way.

You're definitely not alone.

Take inventory of your skill set to remind yourself that areas of your life are going well. If you're feeling isolated, make it a point to get out more and talk to people. The expat community is full of caring individuals who want to help, and know better than anyone else how hard the beginning can be. Treat yourself with kindness and stop judging yourself. Focus on your strengths instead.

OUR ADVICE
You are not alone. What feels easy to one is overwhelming to another. Talk to people and be forgiving with yourself.

WORDS TO REMEMBER

'Practice not wanting, desiring, judging, doing, fighting, knowing. Practice just Being. Everything will fall into place.'

James Frey, American Writer

---

17. Who am I?

I've been here for a while now, but I don't feel like my old self yet. I miss my life when I had my thing... my exercise class, my job, the girls' nights out. Am I ever going to be that person again?

You've unpacked and set up your house... but you still need to unpack YOU.

Not everything from your former life will fit into your new lifestyle. If you moved to Namibia, you wouldn't unpack your snow shovel and put it next to the front porch. You would put it in the shed or garage, tucked away, available if you ever needed it. The same applies to YOU.

Unpack yourself bit by bit and see where each part fits in with this new lifestyle. Chances are, you'll discover parts of YOU that you didn't know you had.

Instead of trying to find the old you, it's time to update, reinvent, imagine new possibilities. With a little creative thinking you can blossom into a newer version of yourself. Don't be afraid to try new things you previously wouldn't have dreamed of doing – you might love salsa dancing, or skiing, or the PTA.

Then safely tuck away the parts of you that don't work in this new environment, secure in the knowledge that when you need them again, they'll be there.

Rather than feel disappointment about how life has changed, seize the opportunity to expand your perspectives. Everything changes *eventually,* but moving to a new country brings a lot of change at once. It forces you to see yourself from a new perspective, one you may never have imagined. Suddenly you have options and choices. You can design a life that feels right and makes the most of YOU.

OUR ADVICE
You're in a new place so you'll change. Don't be someone you're not, but leave room for a different version of yourself that makes the most of your new host country.

From those who have been there

An expat story

"There I was, in one of the most exciting cities in the world, finding myself missing my friends and being apprehensive about making new contacts. The excitement of moving to Mexico City had passed, suddenly everything seemed difficult.

I felt adrift, useless.

It was a member of the foreign community, later to become a lasting friend, who inspired me. 'Think about it,' she said, 'you can invent a new you, you don't have to tell all the old stories about who you are, where you're from – you can create a different past if you like.' I found the idea really enlightening. I toyed with the idea of not being from a large Irish family brought up in Great Britain, but being the child of Russian émigrés, escapees from the Spanish civil war, the secret daughter of a famous Hollywood actor/arctic explorer/Latin American revolutionary/television cook/English aristocrat/Irish traveling family/ Italian opera singer/Polish coal miner... the possibilities seemed endless!

In the end I more or less stuck to my real story, but I did leave out some of the less interesting parts and felt a resulting liberation. The new me relished all that was different around me. I found myself looking forward, rather than back, because what was in the past no longer mattered – if it even happened!"

Clare Doyle – Dedicated Dilettante
& soon-to-be Successful Writer
Irish, has lived in the UK, Mexico,
Belgium & France

18. Finding your identity

It's all good and well that I can be different here and change, but I don't even know where to start. How do I just reinvent my identity?

Your identity is just a collection of labels you put on yourself, labels that make you feel confident, whole and happy. They range from descriptions such as blond hair, blue eyes, mother, and wife, to marketing manager, neighborhood cookie-baker, exercise fanatic or the lady who drives the sports car.

When we are faced with a great change in our surroundings, we often try to grab on to pieces of our identity that previously made us feel good. Unfortunately, those pieces aren't always accessible in our new expat surrounding, nor do they have the same relevance in the new context.

Instead of trying to recreate what you *did,* focus on recreating how it made you *feel.*

If you had a job before or volunteered at the Red Cross three times a week, what made you feel good about it? Was it that you had structure? Social interaction? A sense of achievement?

The same fulfillment can come from a completely different place. Being the PTA president, volunteering at a local church, or taking language classes might do the trick.

The point is this – just because doing an activity in one country brought you satisfaction, doesn't mean that same activity will make you happy in your new home. Instead, look for what you got out of it and try to recreate that.

If you can recognize what you really enjoyed about going to the gym wasn't just the exercise, but seeing people and having something that regularly anchored your week, then you can approach it differently, by supplementing the gym with a weekly social event. Get creative!

OUR ADVICE
Don't try to duplicate your previous life's work and routines, instead, search for new activities that create the same sense of fulfillment.

WORDS TO REMEMBER

'Find out who you are and
do it on purpose.'

Dolly Parton, American Singer-Songwriter

---

19. Mundane things seem so hard

It used to take me thirty minutes to grocery shop. Here, it takes me hours to find simple ingredients. My to-do list is filled with tasks that should be easy, but feel impossible because everything seems so complicated here.

When you're teaching your child to read, the first real words you work on are "sight words." These are simple, mundane words that can be identified on sight such as, "see" "dog" and "can." But learning them can be daunting.

Your kid might get frustrated and feel they'll never be able to sight-read. The wise mother in you stays calm and reassuring, steadfast in the belief that with a little time and effort, sight-reading will be second nature to your bundle of joy.

And so it goes the first couple months of an expat move. What seemed mundane in your old life is exponentially more time consuming now... *until you learn how to sight-read your new life.*

The moment will come when you'll see a weird looking bottle in the corner of your eye and instantly know *it's ketchup.* You'll head for the pasta section when you are looking for baking supplies (and quit wondering why they're together), and in time you'll even instinctively know which shop to go to for a garbage can, new crayons and ink cartridges for your printer.

In the meantime, there's a pretty steep learning curve. So start small. Give yourself one or two tasks a day. Soon you'll find your new dry cleaner, become familiar with the aisles at the grocery store and make friends with the guy at the garage.

For each new accomplishment pat yourself on the back and give yourself a sticker for a job well done. Celebrate each small victory. Soon you'll be sight-reading like a champ.

OUR ADVICE
It's hard in the beginning, it really is! Take it step by step and celebrate the small victories.

From those who have been there

An expat story

"My first big holiday in my new host country was Valentine's Day. The school PTA was putting on a party for the kids and asking for volunteers to bake cakes. I have a great carrot cake recipe, so I figured this would be an easy way for me to participate.

I had most of the ingredients already; all I needed was Canola oil. So off I go to the local supermarket and there I stood in front of a whole aisle of various kinds of cooking oil. Nowhere did I see Canola.

I just stood there helplessly looking for what seemed like a long time until the tears started rolling from my eyes. Why was this so hard? Why is everything so hard? I just want to make a simple cake.

Eventually I pulled myself together, went home and did some Internet research only to discover that rapeseed oil is actually Canola oil.

Back to the store I went, got my rapeseed oil and made my cake, which got rave reviews. It will take some time, but eventually things do become easier. I can now cruise through the local grocery store with ease!"

Martha Klinger – CEO of Kendall-Klinger International
Canadian, has lived the US & Sweden

20. Luxury problems

The full-time help quit, the driver called in sick and our trip to Paris has been cancelled because the workers went on strike. I feel silly talking to my friends back home about this, but these are the challenges I face. Should I feel bad about this?

———

In 1905 Einstein postulated that everything is relative. Time, space and gravity are relative to the situation the person is in. In the expat world, this relates to our "problems."

Relative to your old life, the cleaner, driver and trip to Paris seem unthinkable, surreal. And quite frankly, to most people, they are. But not to you – *well, not anymore.*

You made a big leap of faith becoming an expat and part of the payback is having opportunities you'd otherwise never have imagined. That doesn't mean your life is problem-free, it just means some of the problems you experience are in a different stratosphere. Nonetheless, they can really shake you up.

Just because your problems are luxurious, doesn't mean they aren't problems.

Yes, it's important to keep things in perspective, but running a household in a foreign country is no simple feat, and taking advantage of the opportunities you now have comes with ups and downs. Talking to family and neighbors back home about this is usually frustrating because they can't understand how buying the wrong brand of milk can be devastating or how always having hot weather can be a problem.

But your fellow expat can. They are living life from the same perspective and shared experience you are. If you need a place to vent, talk to one of them.

OUR ADVICE
Your problems might be luxury problems, but they are real. Don't try to get the folks back home to validate them.

WORDS TO REMEMBER

'Problems are not the problem;
coping is the problem.'

Virginia Satir, American Author & Social Worker

Part III
Daily Life

1. Mingling with the locals

I'd like to get to know the culture I live in, but I'm having trouble making meaningful contacts with the locals. Between the language barrier and the cultural differences, I'm not sure what to do.

We know you moved internationally to immerse yourself in a new cultural experience and get to know the people. But forming friendships with locals can be difficult and might take longer than you would expect.

It's not as easy as one would think to "make friends" with the neighbors. Subtle cultural differences can play a big role. Some cultures might wait months to introduce themselves and others will say "hello" on day one. This simple difference can lead to misinterpreting intentions *and you probably won't know until it's too late.*

The locals might be curious to meet you and build a bond, but just as their culture and habits are new for you, yours are new for them. The difference between you is that they're still living in their own environment, surrounded by friends and a support system, and *you're not*. As much as it might intrigue them to get to know you, they can't really relate to living in a foreign country, particularly their own... and they don't need to.

Then there's the language difference. Even if they speak your language fluently, they will speak the local language with the rest of their social network, which means it's hard for you to participate in the grander scheme.

You can still have rich, foreign, cultural experiences. They might come from unexpected local sources, or from fellow expats all over the globe, but one way or the other, you'll gain insights from around the world.

OUR ADVICE
Don't be discouraged – it's hard to get close to the locals. Time and patience will help, but remember that locals often lack the scope to understand your world, and you'll always live a little on the edge of theirs.

An expat story

"Of all my foreign assignments, Japan was both the easiest place to form deep (expat) bonds, but also the hardest place to make meaningful (local) connections. Cultural barriers played a big part and for me the greatest barrier was language. On arrival I spent hours studying Japanese and passing the first level of the national proficiency exam. I hoped the Japanese people, who study an average of six years of English, would help get me to the next, more intimate, level. I quickly learned that studying English in Japan does not necessarily translate into speaking English.

In my second year I applied for a part-time English assistant teaching job at a local high school. As a former Wall Street banker with absolutely no teaching experience I was not hopeful, but got the job, presumably because I am a native English speaker. The curriculum was largely focused on passing a multiple choice standardized exam, so classes consisted of students reading from outdated textbooks (one WWII story referred to Americans as blue-eyed devils), grammar lessons and a LOT of repetition.

Tentatively, I started to ask comprehension questions. My early attempts were met with blank stares, but over time the students got better at answering and asking questions. My lessons morphed into discussions about current events and the one that sticks out most happened during the 2008 US presidential election. A student asked me outright who I planned to vote for, then expressed genuine surprise that I, a white woman, would vote for a black man – an opinion universally shared by the class. What followed was a truly fascinating discussion about race and the homogeneity of the formerly closed island nation (only 1.5% of the Japanese population is foreign). I am not sure if I made a difference, but I did grow particularly close to the students I had for the full four years and when I left there were sweet notes (in English), gifts and tears on both sides.

Unfortunately, try as I might, I had less success with the Japanese faculty and often ate lunch alone. I did not take offense because I understood how taxing it could be to struggle with a foreign language on your break. At the end of my stay, however, I was finally invited to a teacher's home on the outskirts of town and felt in a VERY small part that I had achieved my goal."

Kathleen L'Esperance – Globetrotter
American, has lived in Italy, the UK & Japan

2. The two-year contract

People laugh when I insist we'll only be here two years, but that's what I signed up for – a two-year adventure – and then I want to go back home. Why is that so funny?

Because pretty much everyone has a two-year contract to start, but more often than not two years become three, or leads to a new assignment in a yet-to-be discovered new culture. Postings end early, positions close, promotions get extended and opportunities arise. The funny thing is, when it's time to go home, you might even be sad.

Your children might be happier than they've ever been and you may not want to leave a phenomenal school system. It's possible you discover a side of yourself you didn't know you had, and your husband could be having the time of his life.

The most basic rule you need to learn as an expat is: you just never know.

We can't tell you how many expats started with two years and are still there fifteen years later, buying a home, or have moved on to new and different adventures where "home" is a moving target. It's comforting, sometimes even essential to your sanity, to have a plan, but really, anything could happen. The unpredictability is, at times, both the best and the worst thing about expat life.

Next time they chuckle, remember they're only laughing because they know what an eye-opening, life-changing experience you are about to have... and they remember what it was like to be where you are right now.

OUR ADVICE
As a rule, expat contracts don't follow the initial plan. You could be the exception, but the odds are against it. Fellow expats might have a giggle because they remember thinking the same thing themselves – once upon a time.

WORDS TO REMEMBER

'Stay committed to your decisions, but stay flexible in your approach.'

Tony Robbins, American Motivational Speaker & Author

---

3. Resenting the move

I hate to say it, but I'm starting to feel resentment.
The truth is, I didn't want to come in the first place,
I just didn't stop it. He said it would be a great adventure.
Now I'm stuck at home and starting over while he's in a
job he loves.

———————

Hold up! You did agree to it. Even if you just let it happen, it's still a choice.

Maybe things are difficult, maybe you didn't want to come, but examine why you're here now. Didn't part of you want this adventure? Didn't you want to broaden your horizons, offer something different to your kids and live in an exotic country? Well, you certainly didn't say "no."

When expat life gets hard we start looking for someone to blame. But blame gives ownership of your happiness to someone else and that just doesn't cut it. You can regret the past, or accept the present and move on.

We suggest you move on.

Now is the time to remember why you said "yes" even if your acceptance was silent. Sure, you had concerns, but most of them were based on fear of the unknown and we're pretty sure they aren't the things troubling you right now.

There were plenty of good reasons you made the move. You know the ones. They were the reasons why you didn't speak up and say "no." If you take a good look at those, you will probably see you're making the dream you had come true, you just didn't factor the adjustment period.

The frustration you currently feel is most likely temporary. It might feel like an eternity, but it's not (we assure you). Look at where you're sitting right now. That is exactly where you need to be. Trust that your dream is still coming to pass

OUR ADVICE
Even if you said nothing, moving was a choice. Going back is not an option, so move forward and take ownership of your choices.

WORDS TO REMEMBER

'If you could kick the person in the pants responsible for most of your trouble, you wouldn't sit for a month.'

Theodore Roosevelt, 26th President of the United States

---

4. Traveling back home in the first six months

I'm just itching for a reason to visit home. I miss everything so much and I'm sure a trip home will make me happier. My second cousin is getting married next month but people here tell me that going home isn't a good idea right now – why not?

———————

Going back home in the first few months can give you a false sense of reality and make it more difficult to find your footing in your new home. The first few months are crucial for your transition. It's when you begin to create solid friendships, establish new routines, become familiar with your surroundings and settle in. Going back too soon will confuse that process, not only for you, but your whole family.

We understand that sometimes it can't be avoided, there are legitimate reasons you need to go back. If that's the case, while you're home, make it a point to notice things you *don't* miss. And while you're at it, look for aspects that give you a newfound appreciation of where you have moved. By all means enjoy the trip, just remember you're on vacation and the real home is waiting for you to make it your own when you return.

OUR ADVICE
We don't encourage going back too soon, but if it can't be helped, take time to notice things that you *don't* miss.

From those who have been there

An expat story

"A month before we moved to London, we found out that my father-in-law had terminal cancer. As it was our first time moving abroad, it was already an emotional roller coaster for our family and with this on top, it was just crazy.

We went back to the Netherlands for a weekend every month to support the family back home. This had a huge impact on our kids. They didn't get a chance to settle in and truly realize that London was their new home. During the week it was fine – they were busy with school – but the weekends turned out to be complete nightmares. Especially for my middle daughter – the homesickness was so bad she had huge tantrums every weekend.

On top of that, all our friends from the Netherlands decided to visit us in London.

So if we weren't in Holland ourselves, we had visitors to entertain. We felt bad telling people that maybe it was better not to visit us, so every time we said "yes." We ended up with miserably homesick kids afterwards.

Our lesson was clearly that it is best for the kids (and also for yourself), not to travel back to your home country in the first months. The kids need to get a chance to settle in and not to be reminded constantly about life back home. Also learn to say "no" to visitors, because they will also remind the kids of what they left behind and are missing. Your family needs time on their own to find their way in their new country."

Simone Esman – The Partying Dutch Lady
Dutch, has lived in the UK & Sweden

5. Visiting home

After living abroad for almost a year, I'm traveling back home for the summer. I'm kind of nervous. I mean, it feels like home is here now and I don't know what I'll feel like in that place.

———————

Visiting home might seem awkward, almost like choosing between two competing best friends, but not to worry, home is still home. It's where you came from and it will always hold a special place in your heart. By returning back after a stint abroad you'll experience the familiar with new eyes. What used to be ordinary might feel extraordinary.

One of the gifts of the expat life is that living abroad will deepen your understanding of your own culture and give you a more intimate viewpoint of yourself and others. You'll have a greater appreciation for the foundation your heritage gave you from which to explore the world.

Going home might feel as if you've entered your country for the first time, especially if where you live now is vastly different. Home might also feel louder and more bustling, because you can understand everything that is going on around you and being said – suddenly you're tuned into a lot of information. Take in all these moments and enjoy them, remembering that without your expat experience you would never realize all your own country has to offer.

OUR ADVICE
The old and familiar will become new and different in unexpected ways. Your appreciation will deepen for the place that gave you a foundation from which to explore other cultures.

From those who have been there

An expat story

"The first time I returned home to Turin from Stockholm, I went with my daughters to the city center to shop. After a while, we looked at each other and shared the same thought – how many people are in the same place at the same time. I forgot how crowded the city could be. I had forgotten what it was like to be in my own country."

Frederica Rossi – Italian Mama
Italian, living in Sweden

6. Feeling left out of moments back home

When friends and family tell me what's going on back home, I feel sad. I miss our neighborhood parties and family gatherings. I know they mean well, but hearing about all the fun they're having makes me feel I'm missing out.

If it seems the people you love are carrying on as usual and having fun without you while you're learning to navigate a new country, they probably are. They miss you, they really do, but your life has moved on and is filled with discovering a new world, while theirs is an extension of your old trajectory.

The reason they want to share is because they care about you. They want you to be a part of what's going on, even if it's vicariously. You're still "one of the gang." They don't understand that hearing their stories might upset you, because their life hasn't changed course, *yours has.* To them, they're simply telling their friend about what's going on, so try to see their intention might be to include you, not leave you out.

If you want to take action, invite some new friends over and create traditions of your own. Host a potluck or a Bunco night in your neck of the woods. Start a book club or Mahjong group. Create some fun.

It won't be the same, but you'll be too busy to think about what you're missing. And the next time you're Skyping with your friends back home, you'll be able to tell them about the parties and gatherings in your life too.

OUR ADVICE
Take initiative to form new groups in order to create a whole new set of events and moments in your new home.

WORDS TO REMEMBER

'Everything has its beauty,
but not everyone sees it.'

Confucius, Chinese Teacher & Philosopher

---

7. I have it all, so why don't I feel that way?

I live in a foreign country, we make good money, travel to exotic places, have live-in help, and our kids attend excellent schools. I have it all, so why don't I feel happier?

———————

Because a change like this is big. If you became an expat because you thought "having it all" would make you happy, you did it for the wrong reasons. The temptation is to believe that when you have a seemingly idyllic life you'll be happy. But each move and each lifestyle brings its own unique challenges, sometimes ones you couldn't have imagined as problems. *Even the good life has its bad days.*

On top of that, the family upheaval means your kids and creating "home" are your number one priorities. These are tall orders in the beginning and require all of your focus. But when you see your children thriving in the new comfort zone you've created, your sense of achievement will be incredibly rewarding.

One word of caution: establishing your home and settling your kids is a short-term project. Once you're done it's back to life as usual, *maintenance* so to speak, and time to start looking for another source of personal fulfillment. If you're feeling dissatisfied with life, or that you're missing something, we suspect it means it's time to find a place for YOU in this new world.

OUR ADVICE
It's easy to forget to find fulfillment for yourself when you have spent the first several months building a home and supporting your kids. If you're feeling unhappy, start looking for your place in *your* new life.

'It's no use going back to yesterday, because I was a different person then.'

Alice in Wonderland, **Lewis Carroll**

---

8. Folks back home don't understand

When I talk to my family back home they can't understand how my life could possibly be hard. I have a wonderful life, but parts of it are frustrating. I really want them to understand.

You're asking a lot from people who may never have traveled far outside their comfort zone. It's hard enough to understand a person's perspective when you see them day to day, let alone when you live in a world they can't begin to relate to. They can't connect to what you're going through.

The irony is that not even your husband can quite relate to the way you are experiencing your life. He has his own routine, purpose, and social structure through work. You, on the other hand, have to construct yours piece by piece.

If hubby can't understand, how can you expect people who live on the other side of the world to?

When friends visit, you can show them around to help them understand, to bring them closer to your reality, but they will still be on vacation – you live here.

Talk to your friends *here* if you need validation. They have been through similar situations and won't judge you. These are people who will complain right along with you, or at least empathize. They'll know exactly what you mean, without you having to explain yourself endlessly.

OUR ADVICE
Neither your husband nor your family back home will get the way you're experiencing this new life. Find solace and a place to vent your frustration with your expat comrades.

WORDS TO REMEMBER

'You don't know what you don't know.'

Anonymous

---

9. I didn't think it would be this hard

I didn't expect the adjustment to be so tough. I consider myself pretty resilient, did I over-estimate myself? Maybe I'm not cut out for expat life? I keep thinking maybe we did the wrong thing.

_____

Lots of things about expat life are challenging, no one is going to argue with you there. But if you're tempted to think *challenging* means you've made the wrong choice, resist.

We said in the beginning that this is an adventure. There'll be ups and downs, but ultimately the ride is worth it... it really is.

During the first phase of expat life your head might whirl with incomprehensible languages, foreign customs, foods you can't identify, and experiences you couldn't have fathomed. So, indeed, it might produce some anxiety.

You're venturing further outside of your level of comfort than ever before and very few people can exist there without at least a little self-doubt, but it will pass. The day will come when the sights and sounds that were once so scary will not only be comforting, they'll be the very things you miss most when you leave.

So, what to do in the meantime? It might sound a bit clichéd, but begin by breathing.

Exhale... ahhh.

Look for ways to release your anxiety, such as journaling – some people benefit from exploring their feelings on an introspective level. Or start a blog for family and friends so they can relate better. Maybe take up an art class or find a friend to join you for an occasional lunch out.

Connecting with your authentic self will help you discover that you can handle this, you are on the right track, and you made an excellent decision to become an expat.

OUR ADVICE
Hard doesn't mean wrong, it just means you need to find a new way to help yourself get through the adjustment period. In time, this "hard part" will become a part of the memory you cherish.

'If you obsess over whether you are making the right decision, you are basically assuming that the universe will reward you for one thing and punish you for another.'

Deepak Chopra, Indian/American Author & Alternative Medicine Advocate

10. To drive or not to drive?

 I'm a confident driver back home, but driving here is overwhelming. Traffic is crazy, the roads are different, and half the time I don't recognize where I am so I always get lost. Sometimes I feel like giving up.

———

Don't give up. Getting lost is the first step toward finding where you need to go.

Nothing is wrong with your brain if you can't remember directions – you're just in sensory overload.

Those first few months you can't assimilate everything at once – names, dates, addresses, appointments – and sometimes your brain needs to offload what it deems unnecessary, like how to drive to your children's school when you're late for pick up.

You might be tempted to not drive at all because there are public transport options or other ways of adapting your lifestyle that don't require a car. If you're living in an urban setting or are offered a driver, by all means adapt. But if choosing not to drive limits your explorations, persevere. Blindly trust your GPS, but have a good old-fashioned map in your glove box and make sure a few phone numbers are programmed in your cell to call for help.

When you're on the road, slow down and temporarily let go of your fixation with always being on time. Try one of our favorite mantras, "I have all the time in the world!" Your kids won't be the first newbies late for school a couple times and they won't be the last.

Finally, it's a great idea to get a driving tour from anyone willing to show you around.

Some countries have strict driving and parking laws, while others are so relaxed you wouldn't know they had rules. Rely on experienced expats to tell you the things you wouldn't know to ask.

Whatever you do, don't let your lifestyle and expat experience be hampered by not driving. Pick a place to visit and drive there, then pick another place and do it again. If you get lost on the way? Consider it an exploration trip instead.

Keep with it and soon you'll be the person other people are asking for directions.

OUR ADVICE
Keep driving, even if it means getting lost. Exploring is how you figure out your new home and learn where you need to go.

WORDS TO REMEMBER

'Where your talents and the needs of
the world cross lies your calling.'

Aristotle, Ancient Greek Philosopher & Scientist

11. The big question: what do you do?

People keep asking me, "What do you do?" I end up babbling like an anxious teenager. Right now I'm unpacking, tomorrow I'll man the fort while my husband's traveling and the day after that I hope to find sour cream. I don't know what to say.

———————

We can't begin to tell you how every expat spouse struggles with this. But when faced with *this* question it's not what you say, but how you say it that really matters.

Our role as an expat spouse is extremely broad so it's hard to define what we do in a meaningful way, particularly to someone who hasn't been there.

We're a bit like that strip of land between two countries that doesn't belong to either, a no-man's-land. We're not your "ordinary" stay at home mom, nor are we employed in any conventional fashion, so we need to get creative.

General statements such as, "I don't work," or "I don't really know what to say," not only make you feel bad about yourself, they undervalue your role. You end up walking away feeling unaccomplished, unconfident, and even useless.

You've got to figure out something to say and whatever it is, it should make you feel great about yourself. It's your reality so make it true or nonsensical, clever or funny. "I'm a lady who lunches," or "I watch television," or "I take care of my kids," are all equally acceptable, as long as you walk away from the conversation feeling good. Get your statement ready so it rolls off your tongue and say it with gusto.

OUR ADVICE
Prepare a sentence ahead of time and you'll never walk away from that question feeling awkward again.

From those who have been there

An expat story

"'And what do you do?'

There it was again – the question I had been asked a hundred times since I arrived. It seemed my fellow guest was asking the question to be polite, rather than with any real desire to hear about who I was or what I did. As he turned towards me, I could see his eyes flickering around the room to see who else was around, who else was of interest.

That evening I replied I was a belly dancer. My fellow guest looked a little taken aback, so before he could ask any supplementary questions I rushed on to explain it was all quite complicated, that I had to pick up my children from school, and so I was working the lunchtime shift at a local Turkish restaurant. I have no idea what made me recount what became a more and more complex story – complete with the midday menus – but what did happen was that my companion became genuinely interested in me and our conversation moved onto different areas of experience and interest.

I'm not suggesting one should invariably come up with outlandish answers to simple and predictable questions, but it did make me realise I could be a little more imaginative in the way I described myself and what I was doing.

Looking after children and settling into a new environment demands all kinds of skills and creativity, so we should celebrate our achievements and describe our lives with more vitality, which is more likely to arouse the interest of others.

Did my companion believe me? I doubt it. What was for sure was that we enjoyed a much more entertaining evening as a result of my flight of fantasy, and when you think about it, part-time belly dancing isn't a bad choice for a full-time parent!"

Clare Doyle – Dedicated Dilettante and soon-to-be successful writer
Irish, has lived in the UK, Mexico, Belgium & France

12. I want a job

My friends are content to stay at home, learn about the country, explore and have fun, but it just doesn't do it for me. It's not enough. I feel antsy and unfulfilled when I'm not working.

Being the supportive other half gives some people insufficient stimulation to feel fulfilled in life – they need more. We understand that, but depending on where you live in the world, finding a situation like you had in your previous life might prove disappointing. Language, work permits, cultural differences can all pose barriers.

Don't get discouraged and lose sight of what you're looking for. Like everything else as an expat, you've got to get creative and be flexible.

Before you start looking for a job, ask yourself, *"what is it about working that gives me satisfaction?"* Is it the sense of achievement, the readily available social network, having a personal goal or objective, feeling like an individual and not someone's mother or wife?

Think deeply about which aspect of work you really miss and instead of searching for a specific occupation, search for *fulfillment*. You might be led to a job in a different field or find an opportunity to do charity work or run the PTA or something else you haven't considered. The point is to feel whole and complete and to do what makes you happy.

OUR ADVICE
Replace the word "job" with "fulfillment" and you're in business. The actual job might be different, but the sense of fulfillment will be exactly what you need.

WORDS TO REMEMBER

'If you can see your path laid out in front of you step by step, you know it's not your path. Your own path you make with every step you take. That's why it's your path.'

Joseph Campbell, American Mythology Professor, Author & Lecturer

---

13. The language barrier

No one will consider me for a local job and, frankly, learning the language is harder than I thought. Classes are time consuming and tiring. So I guess working is out of the question for me.

Don't let the language barrier hold you back – you don't necessarily have to speak the local language to find a job. There are opportunities if you start looking in the right places. If you want to work or volunteer, you can find a way. It just might not be the job you imagined.

Check for positions at the international schools, pre-schools or your local embassy. You can often find opportunities for teaching your native language or another life skill. One woman we know became an expat tour guide – get creative and make the expat world your target customer. If you have a hobby there are a thousand ways to market yourself – sell your art, crafts or jewelry, teach a workshop, teach an exercise class, the list goes on.

If you read this and think to yourself, "but I don't want to do any of that," then buckle down and learn the language. You can do it. Go after your dreams. You have the power to choose any path you want. Some desires take effort and hard work, but it will pay off in the end when you achieve your goal.

Language is only a barrier if you make it one. Choose to learn it, or let this motivate you to try something you've never tried before. You'll be amazed at how many opportunities are out there if you open yourself up to something new.

OUR ADVICE
If you don't want to learn the language, there are still plenty of jobs you could do. Think outside the box. Whatever you do, don't wallow.

WORDS TO REMEMBER

'Never give up on what you really want to do. The person with big dreams is more powerful than one with all the facts.'

The World As I See It, **Albert Einstein, German-born Theoretical Physicist**

---

14. This isn't what I expected

I can't believe I had to wait six hours to get my ID card and they don't sell Heinz ketchup. Has no one ever heard about customer service? I can't get anyone to help me in the stores or on the phone. I know I'm not supposed to have expectations, but really!

Everyone has expectations. You can't help it, it's human nature. Each country has its own cultural habits and routines that differ. Your cultural norms are so ingrained you aren't even aware you have them.

It's unthinkable McDonald's wouldn't have a Big Mac or a grocery store wouldn't carry fresh produce, meat, canned goods and dairy products. In most countries they will, but when the unthinkable becomes your reality it's shocking.

You'll always have expectations, you can't control that. What you *can* control is your response when they slap you in the face. Getting frustrated, angry or crying is understandable, but it's a waste of energy and emotions

When you feel yourself about to lose it, stop and realize the reason you're feeling frustrated is because you expected things to be different. This is the moment to say, "Wow, I couldn't have imagined this," and have a chuckle.

Your sense of humor will come in handy *a lot*. And think about it, is it really the end of the world if McDonald's doesn't have a Big Mac or if making a doctor's appointment is a different procedure? Not at all. And if you're honest, it's kind of funny that you expected it to be.

So laugh when your son's sports group has a crazy registration process or when you can't access your bank account because you don't have a job or because it takes hours to do something here that takes minutes where you come from. It's part of what makes the expat life just a little bit zany and fun.

OUR ADVICE
We all have expectations and the worst are the ones we don't even know we have. Learn to laugh when things aren't going the way you think they should.

From those who have been there

An expat story

"We arrived in Sweden in July and were looking forward to enjoying a Swedish summer before the kids started school. To our dismay, we learned that "Swedish Summer" can mean bone damp, rainy weather. There were lots of adjustments.

The biggest adjustment for the kids and I at the time was the change in food choices. Herring, shrimp toast and plain yogurt did not easily replace pizza, chicken fingers and breakfast cereal.

One unusually warm summer day, I didn't have the energy to force something new on my homesick kids. I wanted to give them a tiny bit of home, a morsel of comfort food. But how?

While leaving the park that day, I spotted the solution. Across the street, mirage-like in its gratifying familiarity, stood the antidote for our woes – the glorious golden arches of a McDonald's.

"Come on kids!" I called exuberantly as I marched into our first Swedish McDonald's. The skies opened, angels sang and time stood still as I noticed they even had the kids' beloved Happy Meals on the menu.

After ordering for my children, I decided to indulge myself in an iced mocha frappe. I am not much of a burger person, but an iced mocha frappe was my staple in the US when we made an excursion to McDonald's. "Oh, and I'll have a LARGE mocha frappe, no whipped cream or syrup please," I beamed.

The poor cashier looked completely confused.
I tried to explain, "You know, that lovely frozen
coffee drink? It's more like a coffee milk
shake? Maybe it is called a milk shake here?"
No recognition. My heart raced, my stomach
dropped, I began to sweat profusely as I searched
the menu on the wall for my mocha frappe. To my
dismay, there was NO FRAPPE! My little girl said,
"Ohhh, poor mommy. I'm sorry. I know you were
really looking forward to that."

I will never forget that day. The good news
was that chicken nuggets and burgers from
McDonald's tasted pretty good to my kids.
They had their dose of comfort food, a little
taste of home.

For my part, I came to understand what a
friend described to me months later, 'It is the
expectations that you don't know you have that
can really catch you off balance and make you
feel homesick as an expat.'"

Sandy Nylund – Super Mom
American, lives in Sweden

15. This place would be perfect, if only...

I love where we live – the weather is ideal, the climate is gorgeous, our home is beautiful, but the way they do some things here is so frustrating, it makes me want to start a coup and put someone else in charge.

———

Loving certain aspects about where you live, but not others, is normal, but if you're going into a tailspin with frustration it's probably because of unmet expectations. When so much is different it's hard to see the logic behind the why's and how's of daily living.

To stay balanced you want a certain level of predictability and when it's not there it's easy to feel upset or even superior – like you know best. But if you put yourself on an "inner throne," casting judgment on everything around you, focusing on all the things that are "wrong" with a place, it will start to seem as if there's nothing left that's good. The more you hone in on the negative the more it's going to get under your skin and stress you out.

While there are probably things that do need changing in your country, being indignant about them won't make them happen. It will, however, change the way you experience life.

Strike a balance and find your equilibrium by keeping focused on what is good, what is working, and the things you appreciate about your expat lifestyle. While things are strange in the beginning, in time, you'll get used to how things operate and figure out how to work within the cultural system.

OUR ADVICE
Letting yourself get frustrated about the way things work in your host country will affect how you experience your new lifestyle. Look for things to appreciate.

WORDS TO REMEMBER

'Between stimulus and response there is a space... in that space is our power to choose our response. In our response, lies our growth and our freedom.'

Viktor E. Frankl, Austrian Psychologist and Holocaust Survivor

---

16. This place is getting on my nerves

I'm so tired of hearing, "That's just the way it works here." This place is driving me crazy with the impracticality and cultural imprint that seems to permeate everything. It's maddening.

No matter how much you love your new country there will be times when even your best smile can't endure the bumps in the road. That's okay. We never said you have to be happy all the time. There will be days when even a good attitude won't fix your problems.

When that happens, exhale. Turn on some music, cook up a plate of your favorite comfort food, watch a television show that makes you laugh. Remind yourself this is temporary.

When the moment has passed and you can be more benevolent about your hosts, remember there's more to life than predictability and practicality. There's tradition, custom and a great deal of history that goes into the creation of a country.

If something perplexes you, you might want to take a moment to reflect on what's happened historically to create this norm. Do the people embrace chaos, are they spontaneous, extremely orderly or polite? What are the virtues and values that govern the day-to-day events of life? If you look for answers you'll find the logic, even if it's a logic that doesn't come naturally to you.

Suspend what you believe is correct and approach life with curiosity. Things might not be logical in your estimation, but nevertheless have value within the culture. You won't always have to deal with the way things are in your host country, but, for now, understanding might bring acceptance.

OUR ADVICE
Everything (almost) is for a reason. You can't change an entire country, but understanding it better might ease your frustration.

WORDS TO REMEMBER

THE SERENITY PRAYER
(It's not only for alcoholics)

God grant me the serenity
To accept the things I cannot change,
The courage to change the things I can,
And the wisdom to know the difference.

Reinhardt Niebuhr

Part IV
Family Dynamics

1. Our values don't mesh with local customs

I'm finding local values and lifestyle choices don't always mesh with our own. It can be awkward at times. What's the solution for living in our environment while still teaching our own cultural values to our kids?

———————

Remember you're still the teacher here, even if the classroom has changed. The expat experience is meant to expand your world perspective and enrich your understanding of cultures. Maintaining a status quo, "we don't do it that way," attitude won't expand anything but your chagrin.

Find your optimal balance through *flexible thinking*. When you confront situations where family and cultural values clash, consider ways to adapt rather than resist, but stay true to yourself.

If the local custom is to hire a driver, then you're probably better off doing the same. If you're living in a very safe country, where children are expected to use public buses and trains to go to school, maybe ease up and give your kids some space. If the locals leave their sleeping babies in prams outside the café while ordering coffee, you might not want to follow suit.

You decide.

But ask yourself: if it's hard to adjust to a particular norm, why is that? Does it go against your values or is it just different from what you're used to? If it's just different, then try bending a little to go with the flow.

At the same time, stand your ground. If Sunday night family dinner is important to you, then maintain your tradition. Overly conforming to the "new ways" can result in feeling as though you've lost a sense of family identity. By blending your own rituals with new traditions you'll create a strong family identity rich with purpose and meaning.

OUR ADVICE
Different is not wrong. Stay flexible and strike a balance between new experiences and core values.

'Of his knowledge, a man should never boast. Rather be sparing of speech when to his house a wiser comes. Seldom do those who are silent make mistakes; mother wit is ever a faithful friend.'

Attributed to the Viking god, Odin, in *The Hávamál*

2. We miss the little things from back home

> *I want to embrace my host country and live in the "here and now," but I miss my everyday stuff from back home. The kids keep nagging for their favorite snacks. Is it cheating to import our favorite items? I don't want to teach my children we can't be flexible and adapt.*

Sure you can import a few of your favorites, they bring good memories and taste even better when you're far from home. But there's a fine balance between the excitement of a treat from back home and *still living back home,* even when you're abroad.

Remember, you found those favorites by venturing out and trying something new. Every country has comfort food and snacks, so branch out and visit local bakeries, shops and grocery stores. Ask around and encourage your family to try new things.

Transitioning to new staples in your pantry is part of becoming an expat – expand and explore. Be a little adventurous and before you know it your local favorite will turn into the very snack you'll want to import in your next country. *That's when you really know you've embraced expat life!*

OUR ADVICE

Occasional favorites from back home can brighten the day, but if they become a crutch, you won't have room to develop new local favorites, that later, you'll no doubt miss too.

"'Sometimes,' said Pooh,
"the smallest things take up the
most space in your heart.'"

Winnie the Pooh, A. A. Milne

---

3. My family thinks I'm going crazy

 One day I'm happy and the next day I'm down. My kids don't know what to expect and it's freaking them out. I wish I could control my emotions but I'm feeling vulnerable and confused.

_____

The truth is, your family is probably going through the same thing. They just want you to be the stable one so they have someone to lean on. But playing Supermom doesn't work – you've probably already figured that one out.

Be honest. Talk about it. Tell them about the roller coaster of emotions you're experiencing. By owning your feelings you're affirming their right to have good and bad days too, *and they will likely be relieved.*

If you try to repress your emotions, they'll surface in other harmful ways. Express how you feel and ask for support. At the same time trust your maternal instincts and listen to your family, looking for signs they are struggling too.

Adjusting to a new country is like going through a grieving process. Regardless of how happy you were to move, you're grieving the life you left behind. According to the Kubler-Ross model, the five stages of grief are denial, anger, bargaining, depression, and finally acceptance. Each stage of emotion might flash through your system in any order for any length of time, leaving you an unpredictable wreck, to a greater or lesser extent.

If you're going through any of these stages you can bet your family is too, in their own unique way. Be open. Encourage dialogue. Through communication you'll find acceptance and deepen your reliance and appreciation for one another.

OUR ADVICE
Just because your family wants you to be the stable one doesn't mean you won't have your own adjustment period. Talk to them and let them know this is a big change for you too.

WORDS TO REMEMBER

Hypophrenia: A feeling of sadness
seemingly without a cause.

(It's normal.)

---

4. My husband is always gone

My husband is away a lot, which means I'm left to deal with everything. I feel resentful that he's out doing "his thing" while I'm stuck at home. I know he's working, but it's hard to stay positive when it feels like all I'm doing is laundry, grocery shopping, the dishes and the school run – argh!

As unglamorous as you may feel, your job is absolutely essential. Most expat contracts entail a substantial amount of business travel, which makes the role as the supportive mother and wife that much more important.

Even so, you need to catch a break once in a while. This is where outsourcing and "me time" come in. You need a life too. If household chores are bogging you down, hire a cleaner, have groceries delivered and/or have the shirts laundered. Make sure you're carving out time during the day for you.

When discussing your husband's travel schedule, book a girls' night out or getaway of your own. Don't wait until you find the time, put a date on the calendar so you'll have something to look forward to.

Almost anything out of your usual routine can constitute a break and give you the recharge you need. Sightsee, visit a museum, go out to lunch. Book a night at a hotel where you can rest, read, get a massage, maybe even shop for a new outfit. Take a train to another city with some friends. Whatever it is, enjoy it while he gets a turn to make dinner and handle bedtime. Making time for you will help you feel rejuvenated and grateful, and he'll understand even more why it's important to give you a break.

OUR ADVICE
Your husband's long hours and lots of travel is par for the course. Take time for yourself and carve out time to have fun so you stay balanced and energized.

From those who have been there

An expat story

"It was a beautiful fall day in Athens, Greece – the summer heat had finally passed and a lovely breeze was blowing the sea air up to our seventh story apartment balcony. Earlier that day I'd placed pots of freshly planted begonias and geraniums along the railing. And now, as I set our table outside for dinner, everything looked and smelled amazing. There was a beautiful loaf of psomi (bread) and tzatziki for dipping, feta salad and the catch-of-the-day – white fish I grilled with a lemon, garlic and a few churns of the pepper mill. I couldn't wait to welcome home my husband and show him just how well I'd adjusted to our new country, how amazing I was! Then the phone rang...

It was my husband calling from work. He said he was very sorry, but he had to work late (again), but not to worry, he'd get something for dinner. My heart sank. I felt all my efforts had been for nothing. I looked at my boys, then three years old and barely one, and thought, what do they care about my table decorations, the nuance of a well-folded napkin or the delicate flavors of white fish? How could they praise my meal when they'd rather eat Cheerios? I was angry and resentful that my husband wouldn't see how hard I'd worked and tell me how awesome I was! I wanted him to acknowledge my efforts, give me a pat on the back for surviving the day, grocery shopping at three markets and taking the boys to the park while still managing to get a gorgeous meal on the table.

Given time, I realized my resentment had more to do with my own insecurity about my role as wife and mother. I wasn't the one earning the paycheck or climbing the career ladder. I wasn't sure my contribution at home was good enough. Deep down, I had yet to acknowledge how vital and important I was to the family. As primary nurturer, educator, move coordinator, and errand runner, I was basically the one keeping us all alive, fed, and generally happy. I brought stability and routine to our family. I was amazing, only I didn't need to hear it from my husband, I needed to hear it from myself.

I chose to enjoy that meal and many more I've since cooked for the family table, with or without my husband there to appreciate me. I know even if he doesn't see my fabulous efforts, I'm still a fabulous expat mom!"

**Chloe Heimirich – Mother,
Executive Home Chef Extraordinaire,**
American, has lived in Greece, Oman, Sweden, the Netherlands & Austria

5. My husband and I have started bickering

My husband and I were such a team when we moved, but now every time I try to tell him about my day, we argue. We can't stop bickering.

If it's come to the point of near constant bickering and you can't think of anything nice to say to your spouse, it's time to go out and make some friends. Up to this point he's been a great team player, but if he's the only one you've had on your team to talk to and rely on, then it's time to get a few more teammates. Even if he's a terrific listener and supportive friend, chances are he'll run out of endurance before you run out of things to say.

Before you moved you had a network of friends you could talk to about the details of life. They offered a sounding board to dilemmas, inspiration when you were down or a cup of coffee and a listening ear when you needed to talk. Now the only person you have to download to is your husband, and that is a lot to expect of one person.

We're not recommending you go to the next coffee morning and stand up and shout, "Hey, I need a friend to talk to now!" but we do think you should go somewhere and start talking, start sharing more of what you're going through. You'll be surprised at how understanding a fellow expat spouse can be when it comes to the seemingly mundane issues you want to discuss. Remember, they've been there too. Reach out, look around and your new support network will manifest itself before you know it.

OUR ADVICE
When you first move, your only support person is your spouse. Don't overtax him. Start building a support network outside your family.

WORDS TO REMEMBER

'The time for action is past!
Now is the time for senseless bickering.'

**Ashleigh Brilliant, British Author,
Cartoonist & Epigrammatist**

---

6. My husband seems touchy lately

My husband isn't the sensitive type, but when I ask him about work or talk to him about the kids, he either gets touchy or emotional. If I question him, he shuts me out. Am I doing something wrong?

———————

Don't jump to conclusions. Emotional responses don't always mean something is wrong, it can also mean your husband is simply adjusting to his new situation at work or could be feeling a twinge of guilt that you or one of the kids is struggling with the change.

After all, the reason you came is because of *his* job. Imagine how it would feel if the job were not coming naturally to him or if he were watching someone he loved go through a hard time because of a decision he felt responsible for?

He could be feeling pressure to make everything perfect for the family. He might feel he's at fault for taking you and the kids from your comfortable surroundings and bringing you to a place where you're struggling to adapt to life and schools and friendships. Even if you made the decision as a unit, chances are he still feels a personal level of responsibility.

You might not know what's going on in his head, but you know your husband. Do whatever you know will reassure him that you love him and confirm you're in this together. Your support will go a long way toward easing his worries.

OUR ADVICE
Don't take it personally. Your husband might be blaming himself or feeling guilty if the family is struggling to adapt. He needs support too.

'Don't take anything personally. Nothing others do is because of you. What others say and do is a projection of their own reality, their own dream. When you are immune to the opinions and actions of others, you won't be the victim of needless suffering.'

The Four Agreements, **Don Miguel Ruiz, Mexican Author & Spiritualist**

---

7. My husband doesn't get it

I talk to my husband about what is going on, but I can tell that he thinks I'm over-reacting. He doesn't know what it's like to be an expat wife. I'm the one carrying the weight of this adjustment, why doesn't he get that?

———————

Your husband is living in the same country you are and seeing many of the same things, but your experiences are completely different. When he arrives in the country he walks into a routine, objectives, built-in opportunities for social interaction and a sense of personal satisfaction. He has a job and a clear identity.

You have a job too, but it doesn't come with any of the frills like a support structure. You create it from the ground up. To put it in *his* terms, it's like starting your own company without knowing what the product is.

You have a lot of decisions to make – everything from building a new routine for you and the family, to learning about local shops and enough language to satisfy your demands. You're basically designing your "logo" and marketing yourself as you go out there to find new friends... or at least someone else to talk to besides your kids.

Just like the folks back home have difficulty comprehending your world, so does your husband. He's simply going through this transition from the other end of the spectrum. No matter how helpful he is with shared tasks, the transition of the family mostly rests on your shoulders, so don't expect him to fully comprehend your life. He can't. As the Chief Executive Officer at home, that's your job.

OUR ADVICE
Although you're going through this together, what you'll experience is completely different. Have an open conversation with your husband, but don't expect him to see things from your perspective.

WORDS TO REMEMBER

'Easier said than done.'

Anonymous

---

8. My husband and I are struggling as a couple

 I love my husband, but we're completely out of sync with each other. We're getting on each other's nerves about everything and I'm starting to worry about our relationship.

———————

You're both going through major changes and everyone changes at a different pace –being out of sync is normal for a while. Somewhere deep down, you probably want your partner to stay the same so you can weather the storm easier. *And he feels the same way about you. This can cause friction.*

You're adjusting to a new dynamic in your relationship while adapting to environmental, cultural, financial – and you name it – changes. If you have live-in help you have less privacy, and if the kids are struggling to adjust, that will tax your marriage too – there'll be many factors at play.

But way down in your souls, you're still the same people who fell in love and want the best for each other. So talk. And listen.

Statistically, the divorce rate among first time expats is higher than average. When both people in a relationship are changing rapidly it puts a strain on the status quo.

Now is the time to have those conversations and hone the skills that, hopefully, formed the basis of your marriage to begin with – respect and honesty.

Start by telling him what you love about your new life and how grateful you are for all his hard work. Make sure he understands he is appreciated for what he does. This will open him up to an honest discussion about things you want to work on, remembering he will have things he wants you to work too. Make sure you hear him.

If this isn't enough, don't rule out professional counseling. You won't be the first expat to need some guidance to find your balance again.

OUR ADVICE
Moving abroad is one of the hardest things you can go through as a couple. Communication, respect and gratitude are key.

'A successful marriage requires
falling in love many times,
always with the same person.'

Mignon McLaughlin, American Journalist & Author

---

9. The kids are blaming everything on the move

The kids aren't happy, don't like their school and are blaming everything on the move. They think their problems would disappear if we just moved back home. How do I convince them this was the right decision?

―――――――

Don't try to convince them of anything. They aren't blaming you, so don't fall into that trap. No matter where your family lived in the world right now, your kids would have complaints and woes. They're just trying to find their way. Every once in a while pointing a finger feels like it lightens the load.

Your kids probably do this in a lot of ways, but the big, "I wish we never moved here," strikes at the heart of what you worry about most – their happiness. As a mother it's horrible to watch your children struggle. It's tempting to take responsibility for their emotions and defend your decisions. For some reason, we feel it will make it easier on them. But what they need more than anything right now is for you to be a parent and supportive listener.

If you allow your responses to be clouded by guilt, regret or self-doubt because of the move, you won't be helping anyone. The last thing they want is a lecture about "how great this place is." Just be their mom and allow them to be accountable for their own attitude and decisions.

They're adjusting – it will be harder for some than for others, but they all get there in the end. Johnny will get his groove back, it just might take time *and possibly more than you think it should.*

Meanwhile, let them share and say what they need to, focusing on the here and now, not on how you got here or why. Then gently give them perspective and assurances, as only a mother can.

OUR ADVICE
This is their coping mechanism. Don't try to defend the move with all the positives. Just listen and let them vent.

WORDS TO REMEMBER

'I pay no attention whatever to anybody's praise or blame. I simply follow my own feelings.'

Wolfgang Amadeus Mozart, Austrian Composer

---

10. I am worried about my kids making friends

My kids are very social and back home there were lots of kids their age in the neighborhood so it was easy to have play dates. I'm worried it will be hard for them to fit in and make friends here.

While there might not be as many friends to choose from at some international schools, the kids who attend these institutions are usually very outgoing and willing to make new friends. Most children have experienced at least one move, if not several, in their short lifetimes, so they know what it's like to be the new kid.

If your child is having trouble finding a new best buddy, don't push too hard.

It might take time for them to shift gears and adjust to a school that has thirty, forty, or even sixty nationalities. But kids adapt. They'll soon understand that, "different is the new normal."

Some kids take more time than others coming out of their shell, but they'll discover the friend they need exactly when they need it. And if the right friend isn't there now, they're probably on their way and will be starting next semester. Don't worry.

As for play dates and social time for the kids, each community has a system that works in that country to get kids together and let them have fun. Talk to one of the parents who has been around for a while and you'll get plugged in quickly.

OUR ADVICE
Every semester, international schools have an influx of kids looking to build new friendships. Remind yours that everyone opens up at different speeds and their new best friend is right around the corner.

From those who have been there

An expat story

"I moved schools in the UK a lot so I knew what it was like, but when I found out we were moving to Sweden I cried for months. I finally had a really good friend at home who I totally trusted, and we had to leave again.

When I got to Sweden, the first day was awful. They gave me a buddy I didn't click with and I felt out of place. So, in the beginning, I was anxious and overwhelmed.

But then people started talking to me and approaching me, not because I was new, but because they were interested in me. They wanted to get to know me.

That would have never happened at a local school back home. Those kids knew each other forever, so they didn't need to get to know me. In the international school they were used to getting to know new people so it wasn't hard."

Pyper McIntosh – 9th grade student
British, lives in Sweden

11. I can't find activities for my kids

The new school doesn't offer the sports my kids have played for years. Their life won't be complete without them!

If you can't find the sport they want, consider what your child loves about their favorite sport and keep looking. Is it the running, the physical contact, the opportunity to win? There are many types of sports kids can play around the world, so get creative. Whatever their skill and passion, there are a multitude of sports to choose from.

Start by letting go of, "the way we always did things," and expand your experience. What about taiko drumming, yoga, mammout lessons, horseback riding or even curling?

Also, don't shy away from sports activities in the local language. You'd be surprised how participating in a sport or activity can overcome language barriers, and kids tend to adapt more easily if they are doing what they love.

Keep trying different avenues until you find the path that fits. Taking their previous athletic ability and putting it toward a different activity in which they can excel, will help them develop new strengths and abilities.

Discovering something they never knew they could be good at will build their confidence too. Don't force, but do encourage. Go at the speed they're comfortable with and don't assume what's good for you is good for them. Let your child decide and let them know you'll be there to support them.

OUR ADVICE
Get creative. Find an activity that still fits your kids' needs while teaching them something about their new culture at the same time.

WORDS TO REMEMBER

'A mind that is stretched by
a new experience can never go
back to its old dimensions.'

**Oliver Wendell Holmes, Jr., Associate Justice
on the US Supreme Court**

---

12. My kids are reacting so differently

My kids have been in school a month. Both of my daughters are normally very social, but my oldest still hasn't found a group of friends. What can I do to help her?

————

There are two basic strategies kids use when confronting new situations – the "jump right in" or the "hang back" approach. The "jump right in kids" know how to elbow their way straight into the core of the group. From day one they talk to people, find friends, exchange social media names and create a space for themselves. They're the ones we feel we don't have to worry about.

Those who "hang back" like to observe first, watch where groups are forming and see where they fit in best. When the time is right they slowly work their way in, seamlessly, as if they were always part of the gang. We tend to worry about this type more.

Bear in mind that the "jump right in" group is on a high at the beginning when new kids are buzzing with excitement. After a couple of months they might suddenly hit a mini burnout. They invested so much social energy so quickly that friendship stock went sky high and now needs to come back down to sustainable levels. When that happens, don't sweat it. Give them a bit of space. Make sure they get plenty of rest and maybe add a vitamin or two to their daily routines to recharge.

The "hang back" group – those who take longer to invest – need time to find their groove, sometimes six months or more. Pushing this group to make friends quickly can exasperate them, because they want to feel more comfortable before they jump in. Let them explore, figure out who they want to spend time with and get to know. There really is no rush.

Both approaches are valid for their personality types. Your kids are practicing vital life skills that everyone needs to learn in their own way. Be patient.

OUR ADVICE
Each kid approaches friendships differently. Be patient and understanding, and let them find their *own* way.

WORDS TO REMEMBER

'Life is a series of natural and spontaneous changes. Don't resist them – that only creates sorrow. Let reality be reality. Let things flow naturally forward in whatever way they like.'

Lao Tzu, Chinese Philosopher & Writer

---

13. My kids go up and down –
I don't get it

My kids' moods are all over the place. Some days they say this is the worst place in the world and other days they say they never want to go home. What's the deal?

———————

Your kids are going through the same adjustments you are, only they might not be able to find the words to express their new emotions and experiences. Luckily for you, moodiness speaks volumes. Sulking, marching fast down the hall, heavy footfalls through the kitchen and tantrums are all non-verbal ways of saying, "this is really, *really* difficult."

Watch and listen. See what they're saying when they're not talking. Just keep being there. Sometimes replying in a non-verbal way works best – a hug, a pat on the back, or a squeeze on the shoulder, can say a lot.

If they are using words, be prepared for extremes. Kids communicate with "I hate it," or "I love it." What they're feeling is more subtle than that, but they might like the drama of the extremes. Hear what they have to say, but don't always expect to make sense of it. Just as you and your husband are processing this transition from different perspectives, so are they.

They're young, but they're in their prime of learning. Their worldviews are forming rapidly and that makes this the ideal time to expand their understanding of other people and places. It's a lot for them to manage now, but later they'll have the words to express appreciation for all they've experienced.

OUR ADVICE
They're going through similar things as you, but it can be harder for kids to put words to their emotion. Just keep listening.

WORDS TO REMEMBER

'A child can teach an adult three things:
to be happy for no reason, to always
be busy with something, and to know
how to demand with all his might
that which he desires.'

Paulo Coelho, Brazilian Writer, Lyricist & Novelist

---

14. My family back home is ailing

My father is old and his state of health is deteriorating. My sister is there to help care for him, but I can't help feeling I should be there too. It makes me question everything. I feel so useless in this situation.

One of the most difficult things an expat faces is being far away from loved ones when they're facing challenges. While you want to be there to care for family members, your first obligation is to support your husband and children in your new home country.

Every family is unique. There is no single solution, but one thing is for sure – feeling guilty about it won't help.

Think about your situation creatively, look at all the resources available to you through family, friends and community, and you'll find other ways of helping that are equally valuable.

Maybe you can't be the primary caregiver, but you can give emotional support by being a listening ear on the phone, finding healthcare professionals when needed or rallying support in other ways you couldn't have done if you were in the thick of it.

When you're not directly involved with the day to day routine, you can see things others might not. And when you visit, you can focus your energy and time on the people who need you most.

At times caregiving can be draining and frustrating to those who are on the front lines. By offering your appreciation and encouragement, and choosing the timing of your visits wisely to offer them a needed break, your contribution can be invaluable.

The point is, no matter where you are in the world, they are still your family and you will always play a vital role. It might not be in the way you imagined, but your contribution can still have impact and be meaningful when your loved ones need it most.

OUR ADVICE
Let go of the guilt and look for ways you CAN help. Offer support and encouragement to your ailing parent and caregivers, and you'll still be playing a much-needed role.

Part V
Expat Friendships

1. Can I really build a network in the short time I am here?

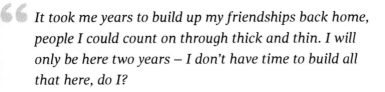

It took me years to build up my friendships back home, people I could count on through thick and thin. I will only be here two years – I don't have time to build all that here, do I?

————

Friendships are built on common experiences and being an expat gives you one big whopping common experience. In the expat world it doesn't matter where you came from, your race, religion, status or age – what matters is you're all in this together, going through the same experience.

You don't know it yet, but you're a bona fide member of "The Expat Club," our way of terming the unique group of people who live outside their home countries.

And in this club if you know a few people you know a lot of people, because we're all connected.

Often within one conversation, or one introduction, we start a friendship. We know we don't have time to mess around so we don't waste precious moments on the nuances of a relationship. We see each other as expats and we know we're already friends because we're in this together.

It goes without saying that we count on one another. We do things for one another that only family or long-time friends would normally do, because we're all in the same boat.

Over the coming months and years, you'll discover the people you meet will be friends you keep for a lifetime. Don't hold back or wait to join in. Go for it and meet your new set of friends already waiting.

OUR ADVICE
The network already exists. It's called "The Expat Club," and you're a member. Start talking to people and see how fast deep friendships will form.

'One best book is equal to hundred
good friends, but one good friend
is equal to a library.'

Dr A.P.J. Abdul Kalam, former President of India

2. Advice is driving me nuts

 Everyone I meet has a tip, or rule, or idea that I just HAVE to do to settle in and be happy here, but I'm not ready to hang my pictures yet or hire cleaning help. Should I do it anyway?

———

Experienced expats have a lot of advice to offer, but what they're telling you is what worked for them. Maybe it was advice they got when they first arrived. Or maybe this is the advice they've passed on to others and have seen how it's helped friends. The reason people want to share advice is because they care about you and believe it will help you.

Does that mean it will? Maybe, maybe not. It depends if you think it will help. Keep in mind though that your fellow expats have been in the trenches. They've learned from experiences and know the tricks. They're passing on valuable information and, we can assure you, it's well meant.

But if you're saturated with ideas and not ready to hear any more, you still might want to jot down notes of advice for later. There will probably come a time when you do want to take advantage of the tips people share, so you know the best places to shop, get a haircut or get your car repaired.

Everyone has the right to their own experience and advice isn't one-size-fits-all so you decide what works for you or doesn't. But listen and thank them for the advice anyway because you might not get around to thanking them later when you use it.

OUR ADVICE
Seasoned expats have a lot of wisdom to share, but if it doesn't work for you, you have official permission to ignore it, or use it later.

WORDS TO REMEMBER

'The people with the best advice
are usually the ones who have
been through the most.'

Anonymous

---

3. How can I make friends?

I'm not a PTA mom and I don't particularly enjoy group activities. I like being around people, just not a lot of people at once. I want to get out and do stuff, but I don't know where to start.

———————

Generations of expats have had the same dilemma, which has resulted in the tried and tested method to fast tracking your support network called the "Welcome Coffee Morning."

It doesn't matter if you attend the International Women's Club, the PTA or a church group, the idea is to meet people with common experiences. Once you're there, you will have an easy place to start a conversation, the "Oh you've got a kid, I've got kid" type of thing.

Some of you might be saying, "Yeah! I love that stuff," while others are dreading any thought of a big gathering. We hate to say it, but if you're part of the latter group you're going to have to get over it. It's a rite of passage. Go.

You have to, because it's where everything is happening. Welcome events are the beginning of finding where you fit into the larger whole of your new community. There will be a variety of women from all over the world, a mix of rookie and seasoned expats, and oodles of information about other groups and activities you'll want to know about.

The big gathering might be where you find your fit or it might be a springboard to get you to what you're looking for. Either way there's something for everyone – a new friend, a website for an activity you love or just a cup of coffee and the sense you are not alone.

Pluck up your courage and dive in. You'll be happily surprised to meet expats who are friendly, open and just like you.

OUR ADVICE
Pull up your bootstraps and go to one or two
of the welcome events. Everyone there is
in the same situation as you, so it's a great
opportunity to make friends fast.

An expat story

"It's scary! Going to meet up with a group of complete strangers in an unknown city. But you have to do it.

I am a true introvert and would be way more comfortable at home, unpacking my boxes, but I have learned you have to put yourself out there before you start feeling settled. Without new friends and acquaintances, you'll never feel settled.

When I first moved, I found a walking group that met every Friday to walk around a gorgeous park. I forced myself to go. I love to walk and I love nature so I figured I had nothing to lose.

I was supposed to meet up with the group on a bridge at a designated time. I got there early, like I always do, and saw the group approaching. There must have been fifteen people. I was terrified. But when they got to the bridge, I got the warmest welcome you could imagine from a group of complete strangers.

The first thing that happened was everyone lined up for a group picture. I still have this picture and treasure it for its significance. Everyone was friendly and had a plethora of questions so conversation was easy. The walk lasted almost two hours and I never had a lull in conversation.

I met a woman who, from that day, became my best friend here. I also met several people who have helped me settle in and feel like I "belong."

The thing is, if you don't push yourself it won't happen."

Martha Klinger – CEO of Kendall-Klinger International
Canadian, has lived in the US & Sweden

4. Do I emotionally invest?

I'll only be here for two years and I'm not sure I want to emotionally invest in friends. When I leave it will break my heart to say goodbye. Isn't it easier to just collect acquaintances?

———

Yes, it's emotionally easier to flit your way through your expat assignment, keeping your distance and turning this into a period of personal development, spiritual awakening and alone time.

Only it won't work that way.

This is where you live now and life comes with all the usual ups and downs that require the support of a friend. She may not be the person you expected and she'll probably appear the moment you need her the most, but this friend, we can't lie, will probably break your heart when the two of you part ways. But it's worth it.

Living in fear of being hurt is a moot point. People move, things change, but friends will make your experiences so much richer and more meaningful. The time you spend with others will create the memories you keep forever.

The best thing you can do is cherish the wonderful experiences you're having – the girls' night out, the book club, the knitting nights (where you don't actually knit), and those cups of tea where you pour your heart out and your friend is there to listen. Let your friends buoy you up during the hard times.

When you move away you might not see your expat friends as often as the ones from back home, but that won't diminish the ties you've built. In fact, your expat friends will be the people you turn to time and time again during your coming adventures. So build the foundation now... no regrets!

OUR ADVICE
Invest! Friends made during an expat assignment are often the ones who last a lifetime.

WORDS TO REMEMBER

'When people are financially invested, they want a return. When people are emotionally invested, they want to contribute.'

Simon Sinek, Author, Speaker & Consultant

---

5. It feels like everyone is moving on

I'm finally settled and have a great group of friends and suddenly I find out that half of them won't be coming back after the summer break. Argh!

———————

Each new school year in this life marks change. Springtime is moving time. It's not unusual for a third of the families at your school to relocate by fall – we're not going to kid you, it's frustrating.

But the good news is a whole new set of families will be arriving soon, a mix of rookies and experienced expats who are excited to be on their adventure.

Okay, we know that doesn't help right now, but stay tuned – it will get better.

For now you can be proud you're settled, have a handle on the city, your home is decorated, and you know where to shop. Meeting new folks and restructuring your social network a little won't be too grueling. It's more likely to keep you on your toes!

And remember, anyone who has said "yes" to moving abroad won't be your average bear. They'll be people who are up for adventure, eager to make friends and embrace new experiences.

Go ahead – take a moment and be bummed your social group is changing and feel sad your best friend is leaving. We get sad sometimes too. Then remember this time around you'll be the voice of calm reason. You'll be that lady everyone is grateful for who helps newbies figure out the ropes.

OUR ADVICE:
This is a part of the expat cycle. A whole new set of like-minded people is about to arrive that can complement, expand, and enhance the set of friends you already have.

SCOUT SONG
(Expat Friendship Song)

Make new friends but keep the old,
One is silver and the other is gold.

A circle is round, it has no end.
That's how long, I will be your friend.

You have one hand, I have the other.
Put them together, we have each other.

Silver is precious, gold is too.
I am precious and so are you.

You help me, and I'll help you
And together we will see it through.

Across the land, across the sea
Friends forever we will always be.

Part VI
The Next Move

1. We don't know when our next move will come

There's a chance we could be staying another year, but we might move next month. We just don't know. How do I plan? I'm living in limbo.

—————

This is one of the harder aspects of being an expat. Some companies are quite consistent with assignment durations, while others don't follow a set pattern and anything can happen. Focusing on an unknown future is unsettling. And yet, what if you did have a plan? Is there any guarantee that what you plan will happen tomorrow? Nobody can predict the future.

We make plans because they give us a sense of security, but that security doesn't come from *knowing* precisely what the outcome will be. Security comes from trusting, from believing that no matter what happens, things will be okay. Accepting life's uncertainty is a much better way to find peace of mind.

Our strategy – plan as if the here and now is permanent... until it isn't. Because right here, right now, is the moment you get to choose. We can't change the past and the future isn't happening yet, so stay in the present and have faith.

Limbo isn't a location any of us like to occupy for long. If you're feeling lost, breathe deeply and observe the space around you. This is home, the space where you live. Enjoy where you are, live fully, and make the most of the time you have with friends and family.

Don't waste time in limbo, living in the unknown. Tomorrow will come, but for now, accept the gift we call the "present" and allow life's surprises to bring you good things.

OUR ADVICE
As you can't plan ahead... live in the NOW!

An expat story

"My story started in 2008 when I realized how unhappy I was in Canada from working, the weather and our housing situation. So we left Vancouver in search for a better life in the US. I quit my job, got my sunshine and bought a big beautiful house with a pool. But again, I found myself miserable and lonely.

I then craved for Vancouver and everything I had taken for granted. I waited and waited to go "home." When the offer to move to Stockholm came in 2014, I accepted it just to get out of the black hole I was in. Little did I know I would be the happiest here in Stockholm.

Now our next move is coming up and we still do not know where we will go – Canada or the USA. Both places I left because I was unhappy. I want to stay in Stockholm where I have made the best friends of my life and discovered my true talents and interests.

After many months of struggling with the upcoming, undecided move, I began to distance myself from my friends so it would make my transition easier. I stayed home, cried a lot and even took out my suitcases to start thinking about packing up. This lasted about two to three weeks. Then I received a text from a beautiful friend who moved away recently. She reminded me of this unique gift I was given and that I must make full use of my last few months in Stockholm and continue living life.

She said, 'I am still mourning all of the beauty and fun in Stockholm, but most of all the wonderful circle of friends. If I can offer one piece of advice... make every minute count with all of your friends there!'

I took those words to heart and turned my world around. I am now taking it all in and doing as much as I can with the little time I have left. I want to leave Stockholm with no regrets, only good memories and lifelong friendships."

Kayla Carter – Social Coordinator Extraordinaire
Canadian, has lived in the US & Sweden – moving to an unknown location

2. Will our next move be easier than this one?

We got a new assignment and instead of going home we're moving to another foreign country. Now that we've done this once, will the next move be easier?

Moves are not linear. They don't get progressively easier or harder. They're just different. No matter how many times you've been through this before, each move is like a first, because it's the first time you've been where you are right now in this phase of life. Your kids are older, life has changed, and your goals have evolved.

How you feel about your next move will also depend on how fast you meet friends, find a home and get your kids settled. It will depend on your expectations, if the new country fits into the reality you imagined. On top of that, it's easy to start comparing one country to another. You might simply like one country better.

On the upside, you know the basic drill. This time you'll have an idea of what to expect from a practical standpoint and you'll at least be able to identify the highs and lows as something you've gone through before. Having said that, there's no escaping the emotional wringer. You'll still have to process the grief and loss of leaving a place you grew to know, if not love.

Some expats have an easy first move and a difficult second move or vice versa. There's no predicting, because you only have so much control over moving into the unknown – you just have to take it as it comes.

Your next move might be substantially easier, but you won't know until it happens. The best you can do is approach the move with a positive attitude and remember that you have what it takes to do it.

OUR ADVICE
Don't expect it to be easier or harder, just take it as it comes. Whatever happens, you'll manage.

From those who have been there

An expat story

"Will the next move be easier than the first? 'Yes.' Or wait, I mean 'No!' I've moved twelve times in twenty-two years, not including when I moved away from home to go to college.

My first major move in life came when I married my husband. We had a few suitcases and an old van. I remember the tears streaming down my face as we drove into Watertown, New York, near the Canadian border. It was cold and gray and many storefronts had been abandoned. I wondered what I had done – I had given up opportunities – only to find myself in a one-streetlight town. But twenty years later, I look back on those years fondly. Once I had conquered that move, I figured I had it figured out. And perhaps I did a little.

Two kids, five inter-US moves, a couple of dogs, lots of furniture, and some additional baggage (emotional and otherwise) later, it was time to pack up and make our first expatriate move, this time moving from Washington, DC to Zimbabwe. The thrill of a new adventure was there, but so was the pressure. I put on a brave face and tried not to think about the twenty-four hour trip halfway around the world with a two and a four-year-old.

I remember many legs of the Washington-Zimbabwe trip like it was yesterday, even though it was fifteen years ago. We rented a day room at Frankfurt airport and then flew from Frankfurt to Johannesburg – where I had an intense case of vertigo. I remember flying into Harare Zimbabwe – a hot dusty parched airport, the likes of which I had never seen. I remember driving in a pickup truck with the kids on the weekend and hanging my head out of the window, like a dog, and thinking, This is Africa! We are here!

So, was the first expat move hard? Terribly hard. But here I am, fifteen years later, four African countries and two European countries later, and you ask me has it gotten easier?

Of course it's easier. I know how to pack boxes more efficiently and am ruthless when tossing out old items. The kids have constant entertainment on portable devices. Internet makes researching a place so much easier and with each move you figure out what is necessary and what is not.

But of course it IS NOT easier. I have left dear friends each time we move and have watched my kids leave their best friends. They put on brave faces as they walk into a new school not knowing what to expect. I have worked hard to become emotionally invested in each new place, despite the fatigue of doing it so many times. I have buried beloved pets in foreign soil. And now, fifteen years on, I am an empty nester. I have had to say goodbye to my kids as they grow roots in a different country while I continue my expat journey and they continue theirs. I have cried tears – both of joy and sorrow at each move. And I wouldn't give it up for the world."

Elizabeth Linder – Full-time Mother, Wife, Sister, Daughter. Part-time Blogger
American, has lived in Zimbabwe, Uganda, Mali, Senegal, France & Sweden

3. Balancing end of school year and the move

I know how to organize, plan and execute a move, but there's a lot going on with end of year school celebrations, goodbye parties and work farewells. I want to enjoy these last few days but I'm becoming totally unglued.

Even without a move, the end of the school year is hectic. Add to that an international move, parties and work hoorahs, and it's a recipe for "overwhelm." Coordinating boxes, parting with close friends, making sure your kids are managing emotionally, plus daily life, is enough to drive anyone mad.

It's not your first move so you know it'll all work out. *What you don't know is how.*

The answer is... one step at a time. One box, one tear, one farewell party, one hug, one suitcase, one minute at a time. We've said this before, but here it is again – prioritize quality time over practicalities when you can and savor every moment along the way.

Sure, stuff needs to get done, but when you catch yourself breathing hard or your eyes brimming over with tears, it's time to go do something you enjoy with someone you are about to say goodbye to – they are the ones to cherish.

Regardless of how difficult things may seem this next part of your journey is going to be terrific. There are folks waiting to be a part of your life, friends yet unmade and vistas yet to be photographed and chronicled on Facebook.

Don't let panic override your fun side. Keep your gratitude for where you are now and your anticipation for the next step in the forefront. Find humor in everything you can and don't take yourself or your possessions too seriously. Above all, be grateful.

OUR ADVICE
Prioritize an experience over a practicality when you can. Be grateful for what you have and remember that more is yet to come.

WORDS TO REMEMBER

'The secret to having it all is knowing that you already do.'

Anonymous

---

4. What can you tell me about repatriation?

We're moving back this summer and I'm excited and worried at the same time. Our lives have changed so much. What can we expect?

Moving home brings with it certain expectations. Be careful. The only expectation you can be sure of is that you've changed and so has the place you called "home." Maybe things look the way you remember, but the way you feel and see them won't be the same.

If you're moving into your old neighborhood you might be tempted to think it'll be easy to slip into old routines or your kids can pick up friendships where they left off, but often it's not as easy as that. You'll look and sound the same as when you left, and people might even think you're the same, but you're not.

You have grown and experienced a whole new world, a world they won't understand and might not be interested in understanding. At the same time the people around you have evolved in their own way and filled the gap of your absence with something new. They've changed too.

Aggrandizing your country or fantasizing that troubles will vanish once you're home will only lead to frustration. If you anticipate support systems will be there and they're not, you'll face disappointment. Keep expectations to a minimum and stay open to whatever the situation will bring.

Just like moving to a new country, you'll have an adjustment period and go through the grieving process. But if you apply the same adjustment strategies to repatriation, you'll be ready and prepared to manage whatever you find waiting.

OUR ADVICE
Manage your expectations. "Back home" has changed since you've been away, and so have you. While life there is familiar, you'll still go through a transition period similar to moving abroad.

From those who have been there

An expat story

"The first time we repatriated, it was by choice. My husband and I enjoyed living in Tokyo and weren't ready to leave but, from a job perspective, it was time to go back to the US. I hadn't loved living in the city to which we were returning, but I told myself I would return with an open mind, as it was our choice to return.

Once back in the US, I felt really busy and optimistic. We had a new house to set up. There were plenty of friends and family, near and far, to catch up with. I was networking and interviewing for jobs. Also, it seemed so easy to be back in the US – people spoke to me in English, I could read signs in the grocery store, I drove everywhere. While I missed our former lifestyle and friends, I didn't have much time to think about it.

Suddenly, the repatriation whirlwind died down. The house was set up. People had been visited. The newness of being home had worn off. My husband was busy in his new position as I was still trying to figure out what I wanted to do next. I found myself feeling lonely and a bit lost – like a foreigner in my own city. Life had gone on for our friends while we were away. Their kids had gotten older. Games and dance recitals seemed to occupy their free time. Jobs had gotten more demanding. New friends, typically parents of their children, had been made. Sadly, I realized we had less in common on several levels.

Just as a funk was setting in, a woman, who had been an acquaintance before we moved abroad, asked me to go try a new restaurant with her. I gladly accepted. We had a great time enjoying a fun new atmosphere and easy conversation about shared interests and attitudes.

As I was thinking about how much fun I had the night before with my newfound kindred spirit, I realized I needed to change my mindset about what being "home" meant. Other than my friends, what I missed most about my previous life was exploring and trying new things. Why couldn't I plan a few trips to have something to look forward to and begin to explore our current city as I had Tokyo?

I started plugging into updates on new exhibitions and restaurants, special events, lectures, etc., I invited people to join us and quickly found out who shared our interests. Not only did these outings give us something to talk about with current friends, they also gave us an opportunity to meet new like-minded people. We both began to see our "home" through new eyes, as just another chapter in our ongoing adventure."

Linda Mueller – Mueller Family Chief Relocation Officer
American, has lived in Japan, Abu Dhabi & the UK

5. I don't want to go home

I didn't expect we'd go home after this assignment. I figured we'd live a few more years abroad before returning to our home country. I'm disappointed and sad. I love the expat life and traveling. I've never had such good friends in my life.

———————

All we can say is that if you want to hold onto your adventurous spirit, you can. Treat this move as if it's another assignment. When you get home, reach out to new groups or try new hobbies you might have never tried if you hadn't left. You can invent a whole new you, even at home.

It's true you'll be going back to a place you know and some routines will be expected to fall into place by the people around you, but that doesn't mean you have to do them, or at least, not all of them.

Go back to your Tuesday night Bunco game, but maybe skip the book club and look for a new activity, one where you don't know anyone to begin with. Pick up an interest that's new and different – keep stepping into the unknown.

Believe it or not, you have become a change junkie. Going to gatherings where you didn't know anyone seemed daunting and stifling in the beginning, but now you can enter a room of strangers and see endless possibilities they can bring... so go for it!

As for travel, having been an expat you now have complimentary accommodations waiting for you all over the world with top-notch hospitality and a barrel of fun – your friends. Just because you have gone home doesn't mean you can't travel and still have adventures with the people you love. They will be all over the globe, waiting for their dear friend to visit.

OUR ADVICE
Hold on to your adventurous spirit and treat the move home like a new assignment. Reinvent yourself and look for like-minded people.

WORDS TO REMEMBER

'We shall not cease from exploration, and the end of all our exploring will be to arrive where we started and know the place for the first time.'

Little Gidding by T.S. Eliot,
American-born British Essayist, Playwright & Poet

Continuing the
Conversation

> *I just read this great book on expat living. It was super helpful and packed with useful insights and tips. It made me realize I'm not alone. Is there a way to help other expats read it too?*

Though this book has ended your adventure hasn't and – for some – it has yet to begin.

We'll do our part by continuing the conversation on our Facebook page, *Unpack – the book*. There you'll find posts with highlights, advice, anecdotes, wisdom – tips and tidbits to uplift and illuminate the expat spouse experience, so please *Like, Follow, SHARE!* We want every expat to know you're never alone. That there are fellow adventurers alongside who've got your back if you just reach out.

Spread the word – add your book review to Amazon so other expats can benefit too. Let us know what advice you appreciated and contribute some of your own. If there's one thing to take away from our book we hope you'll act on, it's sharing your experiences with other expats to strengthen expat bonds and ease the journey.

We wish you the very best on your expat adventure and hope *Unpack: A Guide to Life as an Expat Spouse* will be a resource to help you find positive footing time and time again.

Happy *Unpacking!*

OUR ADVICE
Like/Follow/Share our Facebook Page, *Unpack - the book,* and leave your comments on Amazon review. It will make all the difference. Thank you.

About the
Authors

Lana and Tanya were fortunate enough to meet one fateful "coffee morning" while living in Stockholm, Sweden. They had very different expat experiences and yet their ups and downs of expat living were strangely similar. Discovering they both wanted to help other expat spouses make better and more successful transitions, they teamed up to write a book. What ensued was a labor of love that spanned three years, two international moves, and many hours of discussion via Skype. The real life dilemmas originated from shared recollections as well as the ongoing conundrums of everyday expat living. With advice curated from the heart, Lana and Tanya wrote Unpack: A Guide to Life as an Expat Spouse *to provide hope for the expat spouse when the journey ahead looks dim because, more than anything, they know the expat journey is worth it.*

———————

Tanya Arler

Tanya was raised biculturally as Belgian/American and is a seasoned expat, having orchestrated six international moves in fifteen years for herself and her family. Professionally she is an inspirational speaker, coach, and blogger in the Personal Development and Wellness industry.

As co-author of this book, Tanya combines her experience as an expat spouse with her expertise in mindset, changing perspective, and happier living. She regularly speaks at international schools with her talk *Life as an Expat: Attitude, Expectation and Identity,* offering guidance and vocabulary to transform trailing spouses into Trail-Blazing spouses, and has helped countless expats in her coaching practice over the years.

She currently resides in Stockholm, Sweden, with her husband and two children.

tanyaarler.com
tanyaarler.wordpress.com
tanyaarler@gmail.com

Lana Wimmer

Lana earned her Bachelor of Science in Family Psychology from Brigham Young University. Over the past two decades she's put that degree to the test, raising four children while navigating fourteen moves, eight of them international. Married to a US diplomat, she's experienced year-long separations from her spouse while he served in three war zones with the State Department.

Supporting families has been the hallmark of her career, volunteering in religious-based organizations, community support networks and international schools. As a writer and blogger Lana has shared her insights and wisdom with thousands of expats, and continues to illuminate cultural perceptions with episodes from her ongoing expat life. Lana currently resides in Muscat, Oman, and will be returning to the USA this year to pursue a Master's in Marriage Family Therapy.

sparechangeblog.me
sparechangeblogger@gmail.com

Also Published by 🕊 Springtime **Books**
Bringing Your Book to Life

"Offers a wealth of information and insightful advice on the key issues to consider, and will really help you make the best possible decision."

Helena Frith Powell, Expat Author and Columnist for The Sunday Times

Should I
stay
or Should I
go?

the truth
about moving
abroad and
whether it's
right for you

paulallen

www.expatliving101.com

Also Published by **summertimepublishing**

"True enlightenment for any mobile individual" Expatriate Advisor

Jo Parfitt & Colleen Reichrath-Smith

a **career**
in your **suitcase**

A practical guide to creating meaningful work... anywhere

completely updated and revised

dreams

CANADA

Purpose

SKILLS

passion

Talents

resources

4th Edition

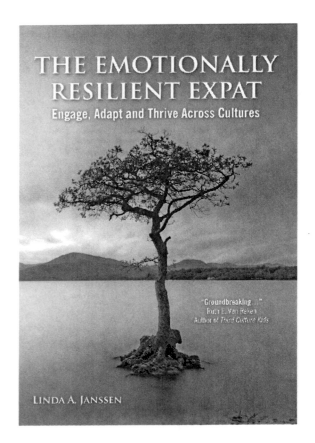

THE EMOTIONALLY RESILIENT EXPAT

Engage, Adapt and Thrive Across Cultures

"Groundbreaking..."
Ruth E. Van Reken
Author of *Third Culture Kids*

LINDA A. JANSSEN

CPSIA information can be obtained
at www.ICGtesting.com
Printed in the USA
LVOW10s2007141117
556310LV00023B/261/P